THE ARCTIC WORLD

THE ARCTIC WORLD

FRED BRUEMMER
PRINCIPAL WRITER & PHOTOGRAPHER

DR. WILLIAM E. TAYLOR, JR.
GENERAL EDITOR

CONTRIBUTORS
DR. ERNEST S. BURCH, JR.
DR. THOR LARSEN
DR. ROBERT McGHEE
ACADEMICIAN A. F. TRESHNIKOV
DR. FRANS WIELGOLASKI

The Arctic World was first published in the UK in 1985 by Century Publishing. This edition published by Century Benham Ltd, a division of Century Hutchinson Ltd, 62-65 Chandos Place, London WC2N 4NW, England
ISBN 0 09 165700 8

Design: Ken Rodmell/Joanna Gertler
Typesetting: Q Composition
Reproduction: La Cromolito S.n.c. Milano
Printing and Binding: Vincenzo Bona S.p.A. Torino
Printed and bound in Italy

PAGE 2 Male polar bears *(Ursus maritimus)* playfight on the ice of Hudson Bay.

PAGE 6, ABOVE Bull woodland caribou *(Rangifer caribou)* graze an arctic meadow.

PAGE 6, BELOW Fall on the tundra: glowing bearberry *(Arctostaphylos rubra)* leaves near an ancient, moss- and lichen-encrusted caribou jaw.

PAGE 7 The St. Elias Mountains, Yukon Territory, Canada.

PAGE 10 AND 11 Polar Inuit rest their dog team in the lee of a frozen-in iceberg in northwest Greenland.

PAGE 14 At a spring camp in the central Canadian Arctic, Inuit tents glow with the light of lanterns.

PAGE 15, ABOVE An Inuit couple with their baby.

PAGE 15, BELOW Herring gulls *(Larus argentatus)* at sunset.

PHOTOGRAPHY CREDITS

APN, 50

JOHN DE VISSER, 37(above and right), 38, 43(below, left), 102(below), 112, 212(above, right), 250(above, right and below, right)

F.A. GOLDER, *Bering's Voyages*, Vol. 1 (New York: American Geographical Society, 1922), 117, 118, 120

METROPOLITAN TORONTO LIBRARY, 90, 95(above and right), 125, 127, 128(above and left), 131, 228(above and left), 231

ROBERT MCGHEE, 53, 206(above, middle, bottom)

BRIAN MILNE/FIRST LIGHT, 6(above), 151, 152, 154, 160

NOVOSTI, 28(left), 143, 197, 218(left), 237, 252(above)

PUBLIC ARCHIVES CANADA, 26 (PA 51467), 51 (PA 53566), 132 above (C 88326), 132 left (PA 53579), 133 (PA 53595), 137 (PA 53606), 229 (C 52514), 232 (C 84686)

JOHN REEVES, 16, 142, 195, 199, 209, 238, 245, 248(above), 249, 251, 253(above and right)

GALEN ROWELL/HIGH AND WILD PHOTOGRAPHY, 33, 39, 106, 147(above, left), 150(above)

KEVIN SCHAFER/HIGH AND WILD PHOTOGRAPHY, 67, 73(above), 75, 78, 182, 185

SWEDISH TOURIST BOARD, 107(right)

VAAP, 40, 100, 149, 155, 179(above), 184(below), 189, 213, 246, 247, 254

PAUL VON BAICH, 7, 99, 103, 107(above), 111, 150(right), 180

ALL OTHER PHOTOGRAPHS BY FRED BRUEMMER

Contents

Preface   Minnie Aodla Freeman   *9*
Foreword   Dr. William E. Taylor, Jr.   *13*

PART ONE   A LAND MOLDED BY ICE   Fred Bruemmer   *17*
1   The Northern Vision   *19*
2   The Circumpolar Realm   *25*
    Photo Essay: The Surprising Arctic   *33*
3   Trial by Ice   *49*
4   Hunters and Herders   *57*
    Photo Essay: Arctic Waters   *65*
5   Early Exploration   *81*
6   The Arctic Route to Cathay   *91*
    Photo Essay: From the Mountains to the Sea   *97*
7   Fur Empires of Siberia and Alaska   *113*
8   Arctic Knights   *123*
9   From Furs to Factories   *135*
    Photo Essay: Polar Animals and Birds   *145*

PART TWO   THE ARCTIC WILDERNESS   *161*
10   Wildlife of the Sea and Land   Dr. Thor Larsen   *163*
11   Plants of the Arctic and Sub-Arctic   Dr. Frans Wielgolaski   *171*
    Photo Essay: A Brief Flowering   *177*

PART THREE   PEOPLE OF THE FAR NORTH   *193*
12   The Ancient Arctic   Dr. Robert McGhee   *201*
    Photo Essay: Traditional Life   *209*
13   Polar Exploration   Academician A.F. Treshnikov   *225*
14   A Changing World   Dr. Ernest S. Burch, Jr.   *239*
    Photo Essay: Modern Life   *245*
Index   *255*

Kodlunarn Island in the Canadian Arctic.

Preface

MINNIE AODLA FREEMAN

OVER THE YEARS (and not because I am married to one), I have come to respect scientists a great deal. Some remind me of my grandmother, who was a scientist in her own right, through her traditional way of learning and through experience. I can still hear her today: "Minnie, do not walk on hard-looking snow, you will only waste your energy; do not eat polar bear liver, your hair will fall out; do not eat too much fresh *muktuk* (whale skin), your throat will itch." Like any other child I used to wonder how she knew these things. Sadly, my grandmother had no way of writing down her knowledge, for everything was passed on verbally.

The people of the arctic regions have survived for thousands of years through their knowledge of the environment. Using their own methods to learn the behavior of the animals that they hunt, they have been able to predict abundance or severe shortages. They have learned over the years what kind of winter or summer conditions they will experience through observations of the land and sea, cloud formations and animal behavior. Today, scientists (though unfortunately not enough) are learning and writing about the Arctic — its weather, its land, its fauna and its people. The knowledge we have gained through the years then, comes both from scientists who went to school and from those whose understanding is derived from traditional sources of knowledge. The information in the following pages has been written by people who have dedicated themselves to studying, testing, researching and writing down their findings. The Canadian Arctic and neighboring circumpolar regions have much to gain from and much to contribute to our knowledge of the far north.

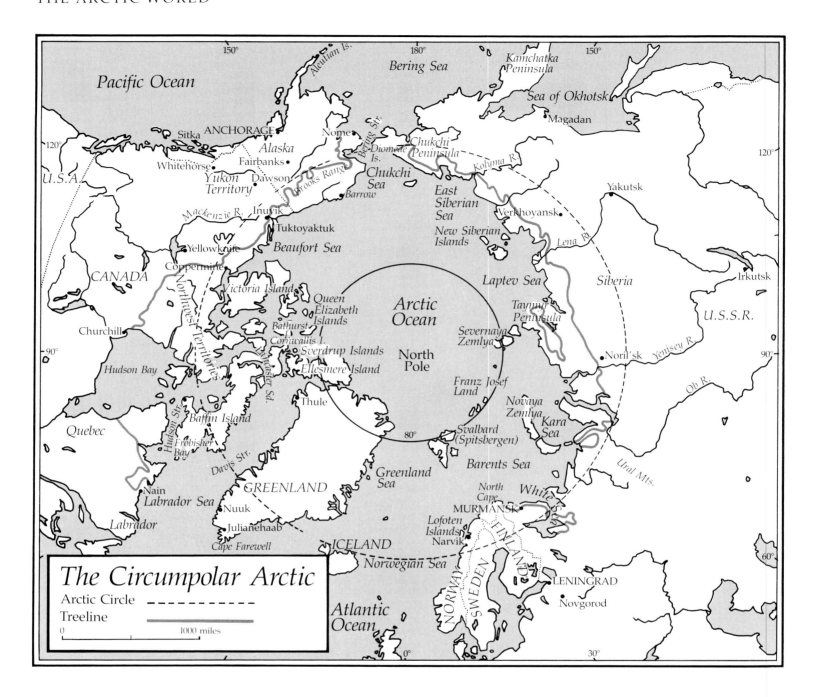

The Circumpolar Arctic

Arctic Circle - - - - - - -

Treeline ▬▬▬▬▬

0   1000 miles

Foreword

DR. WILLIAM E. TAYLOR, JR.

SOUTHERNERS COMMONLY THINK the immense circumpolar world is remote, empty, cold, hostile and lethal. It sometimes is, but so are huge southern cities. Although it can be a forbidding moonscape, the Arctic is also varied, majestic, serene, memorably beautiful and occasionally gentle. The far north is not only a prowling bear, a battering storm and vicious cold, but also a fat bumblebee buzzing among delicately yellow arctic poppies.

Mankind came to the polar world in thin drifts of population. Then, quite recently, explorers, traders, missionaries, scientists, settlers and officials arrived. This northward wave of southern cultures brought traumatic change: from seals hunting and hunted to atomic submarines. The seal, a sharp-toothed predator, gave food, heat, light and clothing; in return, the thankful hunter gave fresh water to the seal spirit. The submarine, equally dark, wet, shining and stealthy, whispers malevolence. Its strange presence on the once innocent circumpolar stage makes the white bear and voracious wolverine seem civil.

This book presents the long colorful history and fascinating environment of the circumpolar Arctic — a stage where people play out the same dreams, fears and joys as everywhere else on this spinning speck of dust. However, in those open, uncluttered spaces, mankind seems much smaller — but intensely human.

*East Baffin Island, near Pangnirtung,
Canada.*

PART ONE

A LAND MOLDED BY ICE

FRED BRUEMMER

An iceberg floats serenely in mid-summer near Siorapaluk, Greenland, the northernmost village in the world.

CHAPTER 1

The Northern Vision

T O SOUTHERN MAN the Arctic has always appeared cold, dangerous and daunting, an immensity of bleak and barren land bordered by an ice-choked sea. "It is more dream-like and supernatural than a combination of earthly features" wrote the American explorer Elisha Kent Kane in 1855. "It is a landscape such as Milton or Dante might imagine — inorganic, desolate, mysterious." The English medical missionary S.K. Hutton came even closer to the popular conception of the Arctic when, early in this century, he described the interior of northern Labrador as a "bare and desolate waste, silent but ... for the dismal howling of the hungry wolf, or the even more dismal howling of the wind."

"Dismal," "dreary," "desolate." The words run like a leitmotif through the annals of arctic exploration until Vilhjalmur Stefansson, last of the great explorers, abruptly altered this vision by calling it "The Friendly Arctic." The Arctic, he mocked, "is lifeless, except for millions of caribou and foxes, tens of thousands of wolves and muskoxen, thousands of polar bears, millions of birds, and billions of insects." And seals, and whales, and walruses — the basis, together with fish and reindeer, of human life in the north.

The natives of the north had their own vision of this demanding world to which, over millenniums, they had become so superbly adapted. They accepted its hardships and gloried in its wildlife wealth, its space and freedom. The Lapps, marveled the Roman historian Tacitus in A.D. 98, are "extraordinarily wild and horribly poor ... yet it is this people's belief that in some manner they are happier than those who sweat out their lives in the field."

The Polar Inuit of northwest Greenland, the northernmost people on earth, live in a region where the average temperature

A three-day-old caribou (Rangifer arcticus) *calf runs across rugged tundra terrain.*

of only one month, July, rises above the freezing point. Yet, said the Danish explorer-writer Peter Freuchen, who lived for years among them, they "believe themselves to be the happiest people on earth living in the most beautiful country there is." The very region southerners found so hostile and depressing, these people called *nunassiaq*, "the beautiful land."

Much of this arctic land has been known to Inuit, to Lapps, and to Chukchi, Dolgan, Evenk and other Siberian tribes for thousands of years. The roughly 200 Polar Inuit of northwest Greenland lived along nearly 625 miles of coastline and in this entire region, noted Kane, "every rock has its name, every hill its significance ... and every man knows every man." The Utkuhikhalingmiut, Inuit of the central Canadian Arctic, had, like most natives, an astounding ability to memorize the geographical features of an immense region. Wrote anthropologist J.L. Briggs, "Every point of land, every rise, every island, every backwater was known and named, had its use and its associations."

But nothing is really considered "known" until we from the south have found it, mapped it, named it. Until then, regardless of how many natives live in the region, it is *terra incognita*, an offending and alluring blank spot upon our maps. The natives left no written record. Most of the ancient knowledge they possessed and passed on orally through untold generations is now lost. Only snippets of their lore have been preserved. Nor did they leave an imprint on the land. They lived in small camps, widely scattered, with an average population density of one person to every 250 square miles in the Canadian north. Their skin tents and yurts have vanished. Their snow houses melted. And little is left of the bone, sod or driftwood homes they built. The Arctic remains the greatest wilderness on earth, and even now the Arctic and Antarctic are, of all the earth's regions, the ones least changed by man.

They were also the last regions to be discovered by southern man, the last unclaimed areas to be divided among nations. When J.B. Tyrrell of the Geological Survey of Canada crossed Canada's Barren Grounds in 1893, a region twice the size of France, "of almost this entire territory less was known than of the remotest districts of 'Darkest Africa'." Severnaya Zemlya (North Land), the 14,286 square mile archipelago north of Siberia, was discovered in 1913. In 1915 and 1916 Vilhjalmur Stefansson discovered Brock, Borden and Meighen islands in the Canadian Arctic. Some of the islands in northern Foxe Basin were only mapped and named in the 1930s.

The Arctic continues to be explored. It was not until 1968 and 1969 that surveys finally determined that a barren chunk of rock

La foule, *"the host,"* early travelers called the immense herds of caribou that formerly migrated across the Canadian tundra. The populations have shrunk, but in some regions caribou still move in large herds across the north.

north of Greenland with the unlikely name of Kaffeklubben Ø (Coffee Klatsch Island), discovered by Robert E. Peary in 1900, is the northernmost land in the world. In 1981, I camped with Dr. R.I.G. Morrison of the Canadian Wildlife Service in a large and spectacularly beautiful valley in central Ellesmere Island. Like thousands of similar valleys, and hundreds of thousands of arctic lakes and rivers, it had no name. We called it "Sandpiper Valley" because it is a favorite breeding place of Baird's sandpipers. On a sheer nunatak cliff surrounded by glacial ice, 12 miles inland from our camp, was a major colony of rare, high arctic ivory gulls. It was discovered by a British expedition in 1980.

The political partition of much of the Arctic is also recent and, perhaps because the north seemed of little value, usually proceeded amicably. The United States bought Alaska from Russia in 1867 for $7,200,000. At two cents an acre it was one of the

ABOVE *Breeding thick-billed murres (Uria lomvia) crowd the narrow rock ledges of an arctic island. On the inaccessible ledges, the murres are safe from most predators.*

RIGHT *Kittiwake (Rissa tridactyla) and chick upon the nest. Kittiwakes, small, noisy northern gulls, like to build their mud and grass nests on the tiny cornices and narrow ledges of sheer cliffs.*

great bargains of history, yet that was not the way the American people saw it. Mirroring contemporary views of the north, they called Alaska "Walrussia," or "Seward's Icebox," after Secretary of State William H. Seward, who had negotiated the sale.

Between 1898 and 1902 a Norwegian expedition led by Otto Sverdrup discovered and explored more than 96,000 square miles of what is now arctic Canada, and under the then internationally accepted rule of "finders keepers" claimed this immense region for Norway. Norway formally relinquished this claim only in 1930. She might not have been quite so obliging had she then known of the vast reservoirs of natural gas, and perhaps oil, that lie beneath this area.

The 23,958 square mile arctic archipelago of Svalbard (Spitsbergen) was *terra nullius* until the 1920s. Norway claimed it, but so did many other nations. Norway finally did acquire sovereignty in 1925, but the 40 other signatory nations to the Treaty of Svalbard have rights of access and exploitation. In 1893, Theodor Lerner, a German scientist, landed on Bear Island south of Svalbard and proclaimed himself "Prince Of The Island Of Mists." He built a house and a road, and had an army of three. However, his imaginative claim failed to find international recognition and Bear Island now belongs to Norway.

All arctic land has been divided; there now remains the arctic sea. Its strategic importance is obvious and its ice cover is no longer an insuperable obstacle. Planes fly above it, submarines travel beneath it, and icebreakers batter their way through it.

The wealth it holds may be immense. An inkling of its benthic wealth alone is contained in the fact that if all walruses were to feed at once, they would consume about a billion clams each day. And there are fishes, and there is oil and there is gas. With stakes so high, the division of the polar sea is likely to be a major challenge, and problem, of the future.

The polar bear's realm is immense: some 5 million square miles of circumpolar land and ice. Rare in most regions, polar bears today are most numerous on the west coast of Hudson Bay.

CHAPTER 2

The Circumpolar Realm

T HE POLITICAL DIVISION of the north is recent and arbitrary. Essentially, the Arctic is one natural realm, one circumpolar entity where plants, animals and humans have responded in amazingly similar ways to the demands of a harsh climate and a hostile land and sea. Borders were drawn by man. Nature is not bound by them.

I once lived for many months on Little Diomede, Alaska, an island in the middle of Bering Strait. Three miles to the west is Big Diomede, Siberia. Exactly midway between these two islands runs an imaginary line that divides two worlds: Asia and America, the United States and the Soviet Union. It even separates today and tomorrow, for here the border coincides with the international date line.

In winter, polar bears amble nonchalantly across this line, passing across Bering Strait ice from continent to continent. Arctic foxes wander back and forth in search of food, and once, in the gray light of a late winter night, we saw a wolf trot from Siberia to Alaska.

In May, the migrant animals arrive and pass, by sea and air. Thousands of whales, tens of thousands of seals and about 200,000 walruses swim through the 57-mile-wide Bering Strait to spend summer in the food-rich seas north of Siberia, Alaska and western Canada. Some 20,000 sandhill cranes and a quarter million snow geese, which have wintered in the United States, fly across Bering Strait to their breeding grounds in Siberia. From Asia, flocks of small birds come to breed in Alaska: wagtails, bar-tailed godwits and bluethroats.

The people, too, are one on both sides of the strait. Both are Inuit, culturally close though speaking different dialects of the same language. Both are expert sea mammal hunters. Both use the umiak, the large, superbly seaworthy walrus-skin-covered

Inuit in an umiak, 1897.

boat of ancient design. They think alike, react alike. Their legends are identical, and many of them are similar to those told by east Greenland Inuit, 6,200 miles away. They use the same hunting techniques. Their harpoons are of identical design, and until recently both used bolas, stone or ivory balls linked by long lines, to entangle low-flying ducks and geese. The border divides them. Kinship and the exigencies of northern life unite them. Both are culturally conditioned for life in the Arctic, just as the plants and animals are adapted in myriad ways to this vast, demanding realm.

The Arctic is immense, 11 million square miles of land and sea, and much more if one includes subarctic regions. The southern limit of the Arctic is hard to define and latitude is not much help. Berlin, for instance, is definitely not arctic or subarctic, yet it is on the same latitude as Irkutsk, Siberia, where winter lasts six months and temperatures can hover at -40°F for weeks. Labrador is not considered "arctic," but "the bleak and terrible coast of Labrador," as S.K. Hutton called it, certainly feels "arctic." The Inuit, an arctic people, inhabit its coast and, until displaced by advancing Europeans, also lived along the north shore of the Gulf of St. Lawrence, roughly on the latitude of Paris, France. Until killed by Boston hunters late in the 17th century, the quintessentially arctic walrus lived contentedly on Sable Island in the Atlantic off Nova Scotia, at the latitude of Milan, Italy.

Rather than be bound by borders or by latitudes, it is easier to see the Arctic and sub-Arctic as four distinct regions or biomes: the taiga, the largest forest on earth; the treeless tundra between the forest and the arctic seas; coasts and islands with a marine climate, such as western Greenland, the Aleutian Islands, the Kurils, and the Lofoten Islands; and the northern seas.

Taiga, the largely coniferous, spired boreal forest, covers more than half of Canada, most of Alaska, 3.1 million square miles of the Soviet Union and much of Scandinavia. It encircles the globe in a nearly seamless belt, about 625 miles wide in Canada and even wider in parts of Siberia. It begins in the south along a line where trees have roughly a 150-day annual growing season, and it peters out in the north at the treeline, where the trees' season of possible growth is 90 days or less.

Dark pines and spruces cover most of Scandinavia, but in its far north birches predominate. It is superb in fall, a forest of silver and gold, the ground carpeted with patina-green reindeer moss, which is not a moss at all but an immensely abundant circumpolar lichen.

Throughout Siberia, the lofty larches rule the northern forest. A gentle green in spring and summer, they stand stark and skeletal in winter because, unlike other conifers, larches shed their needles in fall. Incredibly hardy, they can endure temperatures of -70°F. They reach their northern limit in the valley of the Khatanga River, near the base of the Taymyr Peninsula. There, noted the Swedish explorer A.E. Nordenskjöld, even the hardy larches cede. The last, at the treeline, "gnarled and half-withered" grow only three-eighths or three-quarters inch a year.

In Canada, too, tree growth at the treeline is exceedingly slow. Here, at the very edge of their possible life, the frayed and wind-seared black spruces have a diametral growth rate of three-tenths inch a year — in good years. In bad years they do not grow at all. The naturalist Ernest Thompson Seton examined black spruces north of Great Slave Lake in 1907 and found that these seven-foot-high trees were more than 300 years old. Only in the sheltered valleys of great rivers, such as Russia's Yenisey or Canada's Mackenzie, do willow and alder thickets creep to the edge of the arctic sea.

Violent winter winds compact tundra snow so hard that a ten-ton tractor leaves only a shallow track. The wind's force ends near the forest edge. Within the forest, a deep, fluffy blanket of snow covers the ground. It is extremely cold. The coldest places in the north are more than 1,200 miles south of the Pole, far

ABOVE *An Inuk of Canada's central Arctic returns to camp with a load of willow branches. In the Canadian north, dog teams have been nearly entirely replaced by snowmobiles.*

LEFT *At a northern winter festival in the U.S.S.R., traditional sleds drawn by reindeer are raced.*

Near his tent, during the spring migration from his inland home in arctic Norway to the northern coast, rests a Lapp's wealth: his reindeer herd.

within the forest belt: record lows are -80°F at Prospect Creek, Alaska, just north of the Arctic Circle, and -90°F near Verkhoyansk, Siberia.

Snow is an excellent insulator. Beneath its protective mantle, the small taiga mammals — voles, shrews and lemmings — survive the rigors of winter. Long-legged moose and the elk of Eurasia wade through the deep snow. Splay-hoofed caribou scrape it aside to reach the lichen beneath (*caribou* is a Micmac Indian word meaning "shoveler"). Snowshoe hares hop over it, pursued by big-padded lynx, and Siberia's sables have for such lithe animals, enormous snowshoe paws, the better to run across taiga snow. On hard tundra snow, Inuit and Chukchi use sleds with narrow, sharp runners. Taiga Indians wear snowshoes and use flat-bottomed runnerless toboggans, and Lapps use skis and boat-shaped reindeer-drawn *pulkor* to travel in the soft snow of the forest.

The tundra covers the northern edge of our world. It is a gaunt, forbidding land, yet it can be beautiful. The Norwegian explorer Fridtjof Nansen loved Siberia's early summer when "hosts of tiny flowers burst their way up through the snow … blushing in the radiant summer day that bathes the plain in splendor."

29

RIGHT *With a population of about 80 million, the starling-sized, chubby dovekies* (Plautus alle) *are among the most numerous birds of the Arctic.*

OPPOSITE *A flock of Canada geese* (Branta canadensis) *rises from a northern marsh.*

BELOW *In early summer, the snow and rocks on a great scree slope in northwest Greenland are speckled with dovekies.*

Tundra winters are long and cold, summers short and cool. Tundra soils are thin and often acidic, poorly aerated and deficient in nutrients. Only a shallow layer thaws in summer. Beneath it is permafrost, concrete-hard frozen ground, 980 feet thick in northern Alaska and a mile thick in Siberia's northern Yakutia. The plants' growing season is extremely short: about three months at the tundra's southern edge, three weeks in the farthest north. Some lichens exist in regions so harsh, they grow only during one or two days of the year and then lapse again into dormancy. Plant growth is slow and sparse. In terms of weight, a tundra area produces only 1 percent of the plant material an area of similar size in the south would produce. There are few plant species. Only 350 species grow on Canada's arctic islands. At least 30,000 plant species inhabit an area of equal size in the Amazon Basin.

It is a pauper land, yet oddly rich, for what it lacks in quality it makes up in space: the tundra covers about 15 percent of the earth's land surface. It can feed millions of caribou and reindeer, and tens of thousands of musk-oxen. Flocks numbering thousands of arctic hares have been seen on desert-dry Ellesmere Island. In peak years, there may be 600 lemmings per acre of tundra and, said Erik Pontoppidan, an 18th-century bishop of Bergen, Norway, they can swarm over the land "like the hosts of God." A host of birds comes yearly to the tundra. Only 12 species winter in the north, but nearly one-sixth of all birds of the northern continents breeds in the Arctic during its brief, intense and relatively food-rich summer.

The arctic land is harsh, its bounty brief, scattered and usually scanty. But the arctic seas are stunningly rich. When the least auklets, sparrow-sized seabirds, arrive in spring at Little Diomede, they settle on the island in such swarms that the snowdrifts turn gray-black. More than 100 million breed in the north. In northwest Greenland, dovekies can darken the sky; their total high-arctic population exceeds 80 million.

Despite centuries of often ruthless exploitation, sea mammals still abound in the northern seas: thousands of white whales and narwhal, some 200,000 walruses and millions of seals. The food basis that sustains these large animals is stupendous.

Not long ago in terms of our earth's history, the arctic realm reached much farther south and its animal population was infinitely richer and more varied than it is now. The ice ages shaped the Arctic, and they shaped our ancestors who hunted mammoths in the Ukraine, reindeer in France and woolly rhinoceroses in the frigid bogs of Germany.

THE SURPRISING ARCTIC

ABOVE *Polar bears, as a rule, are solitary animals. But at Cape Churchill on the west coast of Hudson Bay, they gather in late fall, waiting for ice to form on the bay. It is the largest agglomeration of polar bears in the world.*

OPPOSITE *Walruses* (Odobenus rosmarus) *like togetherness. At favorite hauling-out places (called* ooglit *by the Inuit), hundreds and sometimes thousands of walruses sleep packed together.*

*Lapps in festive traditional clothes
at a wedding in Norwegian
Lapland.*

ABOVE *Yakut girls from Pokrovsk, a Lena River town in Siberia.*

RIGHT *A Magadan, Siberia, music school pupil. Music is very important to northerners. In the Soviet Arctic, there are music schools in even the small communities.*

ABOVE *A young Yukaghir reindeer herder. The Yukaghirs are the smallest native group in the Soviet Arctic, numbering less than 800 people.*

OPPOSITE *The Brooks Range, Alaska, U.S.A. The mountainous and hilly regions of the Arctic are often a surprise to visitors expecting to find only flat expanses of land.*

OVERLEAF *A rainbow on Wrangel Island in the East Siberian Sea.*

ABOVE AND OPPOSITE *Many of the old wooden houses in Siberia have beautifully framed windows.*

OVERLEAF *An Inuit camp at night at Aberdeen Bay on southern Baffin Island, Canada. Inuit from several settlements gather at this remote bay to mine soapstone from a nearby deposit for carvings.*

ABOVE *Aleuts attend a service in a Russian Orthodox church in Alaska. Converted by Russian priests when Alaska still belonged to Russia, most Aleuts still belong to the Orthodox faith.*

OPPOSITE *After sewing a sealskin cover onto a new kayak, a Polar Inuit woman of Greenland rests and smokes her pipe.*

OVERLEAF *An Inuit girl of Canada's central Arctic, her face framed by a ruff of wolverine fur.*

CHAPTER 3

Trial by Ice

EIGHTEEN THOUSAND YEARS AGO, a mere instant of geological time, one-third of the earth's land surface was covered by mile-thick ice. Ice shaped the northern lands, and cold shaped northern man.

Mankind was born in warmth, presumably in Africa, and was not designed by nature to cope with cold. Naked humans are comfortable at an air temperature of 75°F; our normal body temperature is 98.6°F. We are the naked apes of balmy climes and, biologically speaking, the north is not the place for us. If our body's core temperature is lowered by only 9°F, our thermo-regulatory system begins to falter and death is near. A naked human exposed to −40°F and winds of 20 miles per hour — conditions common in the Arctic — would die in 15 minutes.

When the ice age climate descended upon early man, he had to flee, adapt or perish. Some may have fled and others, no doubt, perished as the climate cooled and glaciers ground south-ward. But some remained and learned to live with cold. The physiological adaptation was probably minor. Like Inuit and Chukchi, they may have had small hands and feet and a higher basal metabolic rate than people in warm lands. But there sim-ply was not enough time to develop a truly arctic, cold-resistant, densely furred human strain. Instead, brainy humans devel-oped a cold-adapted culture.

They built shelters of animal bones and skins, or moved into caves, evicting such formidable occupants as cave bears or cave lions. They made fires to warm and protect their lairs, and they dressed in the marvelously warm furs of cold-adapted animals. They invented tools — stone knives, axes and awls, bone needles and scrapers, wood-shafted spears and, even more ingenious and deadly, the spear thrower which, using the lever principle, more than tripled the hunter's throwing force.

In the summer, traditional Nenets chooms, tents of skin or bark, *are still used in the Russian Arctic.*

They tackled all animals, from marmot to mammoth. They used the stealthy stalk and the clever ambush. They used fire to stampede and kill their prey. They chased wild horses over cliffs, and they mired mammoths in bogs. Ice age man hunted alone or, more often, in coordinated effort with other men of his group. He was puny but shrewd, "a cunning hunter" as the Bible says of Esau, and it was this cunning and inventiveness that enabled him to survive the times when the Arctic reached far to the south.

At least four times during the two-and-a-half million years of the Pleistocene, giant ice sheets spread out from the north, and four times, during warm interglacial periods, they receded. Cold-loving animals moved northward with the retreating tundras and warmth-loving animals reestablished residence in regions from which the cold had expelled them: 130,000 years ago, lions roamed across France and hippopotamuses lolled in the Thames.

About 125,000 years ago, the last ice age began. In the north, snowfall exceeded annual melt. The snows of yesteryear remained upon the land, turned into coarse-grained firn and were covered by the snows of succeeding winters. Year by year the layer increased and compressed into glacial ice that finally attained a thickness of three miles upon parts of northern Canada.

Yielding to the pressure of this billion-ton burden, the stupendous ice sheets moved outward from initial core areas and oozed across the land. At the peak of the last ice age, 18,000 years ago, ice sheets covered nearly all of Canada and large portions of the northern United States. In Europe, the icy juggernaut crushed Scandinavia and crept onward across northwestern Russia, northern Germany, Scotland and most of England and Ireland. Other ice sheets formed on the mountains, and great glaciers descended from the Alps and Pyrenees far into the lowlands. Worldwide, an area four times the size of present-day Europe was covered by ice. Of the northern lands, only a small portion of northwestern Canada, parts of Alaska and most of Siberia were free of ice.

It was cold, windy and dry. Fierce storms screamed down the ice caps, scooped up dry earth from the edges of the glaciers and scattered this fertile loess far across the periglacial plains. Although it was cool in summer and cold in winter, the climate of the ice-free regions was clement enough and the earth rich enough to produce an extensive vegetation that fed the greatest array of large mammals the earth has ever known.

For this was the age of giants. Herds of thick-furred woolly mammoths roamed the tundra, sweeping aside the snow with immense curved tusks to get at the vegetation beneath. They

A group of Aivillik Inuit in a large snow house, 1905.

were so numerous that in Russia alone the remains of more than 117,000 mammoths have been found, and half of the world's ivory comes from their imperishable tusks. Woolly rhinoceroses with three-foot-long horns fed in the marshes, and ungainly, knobby-kneed camels, much larger than any camel today, paced over the plains. Ranging as far north as Alaska, the tiny-brained megatherium, a two-story-high ground sloth, munched placidly but nearly continuously on foliage to keep its enormous body stoked.

Fearsome predators pursued the plant eaters: thick-furred cave lions, larger than present-day lions; seven-foot-long dire wolves, fast and deadly; huge, long-legged bears; and saber-toothed cats that stabbed their prey with bayonet-long fangs. And man, first Neanderthal man and then Cro-Magnon man, short of tooth and claw, but more deadly than any of the other predators.

Neanderthal people were spread sparsely across much of the earth: their remains have been found from Germany to Africa and from Belgium to China and Java. They lived in Europe when the last ice age began and evolved a culture well adapted to cold.

51

Motionless, his harpoon at the ready, a fur-clad Polar Inuk of northwest Greenland stands on the ice of Inglefield Bay waiting for a ringed seal to surface in its breathing hole.

The first remains of these prehistoric humans were found in 1856 in the Neanderthal Valley, not far from Düsseldorf. Neanderthal man quickly acquired a poor reputation: he was usually depicted as a brutish, beetle-browed, hirsute moron who clubbed bears and his mate into submission, grunted "ugh" and dragged them to his lair. He was the archetypal caveman.

He did live in caves where caves existed; they were the logical shelter when snow fell and winds howled. But he was not stupid or he would never have survived the trial by cold of the ice ages. Neanderthal man invented, improved or perfected a multitude of tools and weapons. He made tents of animal skins and weighed the lower flaps with stones, as people in the north do to this day. He hunted with club, spear and bola. He made fur clothing to protect himself from the cold. He killed the mighty cave bear but also worshiped it; it is perhaps to him, 60,000 years ago and more, that we can trace the bear veneration

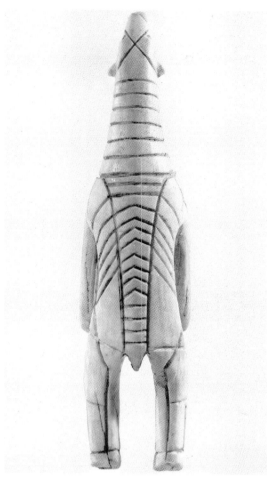

An ivory carving of a bear from the Dorset culture (800 B.C.–A.D. *1000) found near Igloolik, Canada.*

of nearly all northern peoples, from Lapps to Inuit. He knew love and compassion, for he took care of the old and the crippled who could no longer hunt. He believed in an afterlife, for he buried gifts with his dead and scattered bright flowers into their graves. And he killed his foes and ate them. He was, in short, a very human human.

Neanderthal man's reign lasted for nearly 100,000 years and then, in less than 5,000 years, he vanished — supplanted, eliminated or absorbed by an even more intelligent successor: Cro-Magnon man.

This thoroughly "modern" human, *Homo sapiens*, adopted, adapted or invented nearly the entire arsenal of weapons, tools and stratagems used by northern hunters until recently, and in some instances until the present day. He invented the eyed needle and made excellent fur clothing. He caught salmon in stone weirs similar to the *sapotit* built by Inuit and speared the fish with trident-like leisters similar to those used by some Inuit to this day. He played a game of chance with the tarsal bones of animals, closely akin to the *inukat* bone game of the Inuit. And, like the Inuit and other northern peoples, he knew how to strike fire with pyrite and flint.

Cro-Magnon people roamed the world, for in their time the world was nearly one. Locked within the monstrous ice sheets that covered a third of all land were 17 million cubic miles of water. This, ultimately, came from the world's oceans, and their level was then about 400 feet lower than it is now. Sri Lanka was then a part of India; Japan and Sakhalin Island were attached to the Asian mainland; and a 1,000-mile-wide land bridge connected Asia and North America. Across this giant causeway animals, plants and man moved from continent to continent and to this, in large part, is due the great similarity of the circumpolar arctic fauna and flora. From America to Eurasia went horse and camel, and at different times of the Pleistocene there came to America from Eurasia musk-ox, moose, bison, caribou, beaver, lion and chipmunk. And man, too, came from Asia and spread across the empty continent, from Alaska to Tierra del Fuego.

The ice sheets maintained briefly their farthest advance and then, for reasons still not fully understood, the climatic pendulum began to swing again toward renewed warmth. The mountain-high ice masses crumbled, melted, receded. Torrents of silt-laden meltwater rushed to the sea, and the level of the world's oceans began to rise again. Lichens and mosses, the hardy pioneers of the plant world, settled the sodden, till-strewn land left by the retreating ice. Higher plants followed, and finally the forests moved northward again.

Plants prospered, but the Pleistocene megafauna, the most marvelous assemblage of mighty mammals that ever existed, declined and vanished. It seems nearly certain that it was puny, cunning man who hastened their demise. The house-high sloth, the giant elk, the mastodon, the mammoth and hundreds more perished, their massive bones and tusks mute witness to their long-ago existence. "Mammout's tusks are found about the Siberian rivers and the shores of the Icy Sea, and scattered all over the arctic flats," wrote the explorer Martin Sauer, who spent nine years (1785–1794) in Siberia. "It appears that the animal is extinct."

The giants faded away slowly in Eurasia but died out with stunning abruptness in North America, where most vanished in about 1,000 years. Most of the great plant eaters had lived either near the edge of the northern forest or on the open tundra and steppe. They were not forest animals. As the ice receded, the forest advanced, and as the ice melted, the ocean levels rose. Caught between encroaching forest and the rising sea, their range drastically reduced, the great herbivores may have had trouble finding the vast mass of fodder their huge bulks required. Each mammoth needed about 250 pounds of plants a day.

If hostile nature reduced the giants' food and range, it was probably man who pushed them over the brink into the eternal abyss of extinction. When humans crossed from Eurasia into America, they came into an Eden that had never known man. Perhaps the Goliaths of the animal world simply did not take these little beings seriously. But man had slings, bows and arrows, spears, fire and ingenious traps. Musk-oxen, to this day, when confronted by man behave as if humans were wolves. They stand shoulder to shoulder, sharp-horned heads turned toward the enemy. It is an excellent stratagem against wolves. It is suicidal when confronted by armed men. Musk-oxen died out in Europe thousands of years ago, persisted in Siberia until about 2,000 years ago, and were exterminated in Alaska in 1865. They survived only in the remote regions of arctic Canada and Greenland (they have since been reintroduced in Alaska and Eurasia).

The gentle sirenian of the north, the 33-foot-long Steller's sea cow, may once have had an extensive range. Perhaps adverse climatic conditions, and perhaps early man, or probably both, reduced this range until, when they were discovered by the Russian explorer Vitus Bering in 1741, they were confined to the shallow waters near the uninhabited Commander Islands off Kamchatka. Bering's hungry men killed some sea cows and found they tasted like beef. Discovered in 1741, the last of these

Musk-oxen (Ovibos moschatus) *stand shoulder to shoulder to ward off an enemy. A perfect strategem against wolves, this defensive position was suicidal when musk-oxen faced armed men.*

huge, herbivorous sea creatures was killed in 1768.

And thus, perhaps, the ice age giants died, their range diminished, their numbers decimated by man, the ultimate predator. Their very size may have hastened their downfall: one mammoth made a mighty meal, and hunters may have been eager to expend great energy and incur great risks to slay one of these huge beasts.

Since that drastic destruction by nature and man, few northern animals have died out and those but recently: the spectacled cormorant around 1820, the great auk in 1844, the Labrador duck in 1875. The others, the arctic animals of today, lived in uneasy balance with invading man. Perhaps they were better suited than the ice age giants to coexist with man. Perhaps arctic man had not the means or will to eradicate them. Perhaps he consciously avoided exterminating the animals upon which his life depended. A recurrent theme in early Alaskan native art is a hand with a large hole in its palm. It symbolizes the ancient creed that a hunter must let some prey escape, or else none will survive and he, too, will perish.

Ringed seals have many breathing holes. In former days, when hunting was vital, men stood at holes without moving for hours, even for days.

CHAPTER 4

Hunters and Herders

O F ALL THE EARTH'S REGIONS the Arctic is perhaps the most hostile and potentially most lethal environment ever inhabited by humans. On northern Ellesmere Island and in Peary Land, north Greenland, where Inuit once lived, the mean January temperature is -29°F, winter storms are frequent, and the sun sets in mid-October and does not rise above the horizon again until early March. Since this does not seem alluring, the question naturally arises: why did people settle there? The answer is probably two-fold: it was a haven and a refuge from enemies, and it was relatively rich in game.

The oral tradition of many arctic Eurasian people contains a common theme: long ago, they lived much farther south and their ancestors fled northward to escape persecution by more powerful, warlike neighbors. The Lapps' forebears, scientists believe, once lived in northwestern Russia. The log houses of arctic Yakuts are of a distinctively southern design, and the Evenk habit of riding reindeer is believed to hark back to southern ancestors who rode horses. When the Inuit's remote forebears came to America, nearly the entire continent, except the Arctic, had been preempted by the Indians' ancestors. Their way south barred by resident and probably hostile tribes, the proto-Inuit moved eastward along the empty, harsh but game-rich arctic coast.

For a hunting people culturally adapted to cold, the Arctic had its attractions: millions of caribou and reindeer, tens of thousands of musk-oxen, millions of birds and seals, hundreds of thousands of whales and walruses, and an abundance of fish in rivers and lakes. When the English explorer Samuel Hearne crossed Canada's Barren Grounds in 1771, he often saw "many herds [of musk-oxen] in the course of a day's walk,

Drifting snow in spring lies packed against the fur hood and face of a young Inuit girl.

and some of those herds did not contain less than eighty or an hundred head.'' Another explorer, I.I. Hayes, saw walruses near Etah, northwest Greenland; the pack ice was covered with them ''as far as the eye could reach.'' Some subarctic regions were even richer. The Russian writer Anton Chekhov spent many months on Sakhalin Island in 1890 and marveled at its wildlife wealth. In spring the herring ran, ''the sea appears to be boiling over ... and the number of whales, following the herring ... is so great that [the explorer] Krusenstern's ship was encircled by them ...'' and could reach shore only ''with extreme caution.'' Such animal concentrations were, of course, local and seasonal, but compared, for instance, with the north's vast forest belt, the arctic seas and tundra were rich in game.

Among the peoples of the north, there was a fairly sharp division between those who hunted caribou or reindeer and those who hunted sea mammals. There were, for example, the mountain and forest Lapps, who were both reindeer hunters (and later breeders), and the coast Lapps, who fished and hunted seals. Most Nenets (formerly called ''Samoyeds,'' a term they understandably detest since it means ''cannibal'' in Russian) were reindeer people, but those along the coast hunted seal, walrus and white whale. Most Inuit were sea mammal hunters. But the existence of Alaska's Nunamiut (the ''land'' or ''inland'' people) and of the Caribou Inuit of Canada's Barrens was nearly totally centered upon caribou.

These Inuit lived primarily on caribou meat and fat. Their clothes were made of caribou skins, and most of their tools, weapons and toys were made of caribou antler or bone. Had the world been created with but one animal, the caribou, they probably would have been content, for it provided them with all their needs. I once lived with an old Inuk caribou hunter and his family, and for weeks in spring our world revolved around *tuktu*, ''the caribou.'' The people hunted caribou, ate caribou and talked endlessly of caribou. They even dreamed of caribou. At night, the older hunter muttered in his sleep, and it was *tuktu*, always *tuktu*, great herds of caribou wandering through his dreams.

It was the same another spring when I lived with the Lapps. Only there the talk was of reindeer. One-fourth of all words in the language of Swedish Lapps pertains to reindeer and to reindeer herding and breeding. Long ago, they thought of *saivo* (''heaven'') as a place much like this earth only with infinitely more reindeer.

There was, however, one fundamental difference between the people with whom I lived: the Inuit were caribou hunters, the Lapps were reindeer herders. In the beginning, arctic people

RIGHT *Inuit camp in a snowstorm. In the past, when it was too stormy to hunt, people would visit one another.*

BELOW *Sled dogs sleep in a storm near an Inuit camp in the Canadian Arctic. Curled up tightly, the dogs let themselves be covered by a blanket of snow. In this way, they are able to survive the cold and blizzards of the Arctic.*

A hunter from Grise Fiord on Ellesmere Island, Canada's northernmost settlement, returns with a shot caribou to his hunting camp on Devon Island.

were reindeer hunters. They killed them with bow and arrow; they speared them from boats as they crossed rivers; they built *inukshuit*, alignments of man-shaped cairns to shoo the migrating animals toward hidden hunters; and they caught them in ingenious snow traps baited with urine. And from Lapland to Labrador, they herded wild reindeer into pounds, large enclosures in the forest built with felled trees and brush, where they were caught in thong snares and easily killed. As Samuel Hearne noted in 1771, "This method of hunting is so successful that many families of Northern Indians subsist by it all winter." Some pounds were enormous. In 1983, I flew over one in the remote and now uninhabited region near Lac Rendezvous in the northwestern Canadian Arctic. The pound's circumference was at least three miles. Built perhaps centuries ago, the giant trap was still clearly visible from the air.

At least 2,000 years ago, some shrewd arctic Eurasian, probably a Lapp, took the pound idea one step further. He did not kill all of the reindeer in his trap, but kept a few, tamed them and used them as decoys to lure their wild brethren into the enclosure. In the late 9th century the Norse chieftain Ottar visited King Alfred the Great of England and told him about his travels and his wealth. He owned "600 tame Deere … which they call Rane Deere." Six of them were "stall Rane Deere, a beast of great value, and marveilously esteemed among the Fynnes [Lapps], for that with them they catch the wilde Rane Deere."

They began with a few decoy reindeer and progressed to keeping herds of tame reindeer. Reindeer husbandry became the basis of life for most people of northern Eurasia. Explorer Fridtjof Nansen painted a vivid, though idealized, picture of the Siberian reindeer herder's life in 1893: "And over these mighty tundra plains of Asia … the nomad wanders with his reindeer herds, a glorious free life. Where he wills, he pitches his tent, his reindeer around him; and at his will he goes on his way … He has no goal to struggle towards, no anxieties to endure — he has merely to live." That life was often hard and sometimes dangerous. But it did provide a measure of certainty and security, and in Eurasia it remains important to this day. More than two-and-a-half million reindeer are kept in the Soviet Union and another million are herded in northern Scandinavia.

In prehistoric time the reindeer culture ended abruptly at Bering Strait, and modern attempts to transplant reindeer and reindeer husbandry to North America have had little success. Siberian reindeer were brought to Alaska in 1890, increased rapidly, overbrowsed the limited range upon which they were kept and declined drastically. A large reindeer herd was driven

Reindeer rush past a Lapp herder during a fall roundup in arctic Norway. Animals to be marked or slaughtered are caught with a lasso.

from Alaska to Canada's Mackenzie River delta in the 1930s. It was an epic five-year trek, and then the reindeer and the "reindeer project" became the neglected wards of a distant government agency. Now privately owned, the reindeer herd's main value consists of its antlers, which are sold in the Orient for a high price as supposedly potent restorers of flagging virility.

The main obstacle to successful reindeer breeding in North America was not inexperience or government bungling, but the natives' near-total disinterest. The herder's life did not appeal to Inuit. They were exceedingly skillful sea mammal hunters with a unique culture that had honed to perfection the art of survival in the Arctic.

It took millenniums to attain this perfection. Just when and where the Inuit originated are subjects of conjecture. People of Arctic Mongoloid stock probably came from Siberia across Bering Strait to Alaska about 10,000 years ago, and many scientists believe they were the distant ancestors of both Inuit and Aleuts.

From these hazy figures of the remote past came the people of the Arctic Small Tool Tradition. They spread eastward from Alaska about 5,000 years ago across the Arctic all the way north to Ellesmere Island and east to east Greenland, leaving delicately chipped stone tools and small rock hearths on the beaches of the farthest north. Their life must have been one of unbelievable hardship. They had no boats, no sleds, no dog teams. There is no evidence that they had oil lamps or igloos. They probably lived summer and winter in small, poorly heated tents in a region where winter lasts nine months. Yet somehow, despite such terrifying odds, they persisted, a few thousand people scattered across the immensity of the north.

From these people of the Arctic Small Tool Tradition other cultures evolved — the Pre-Dorset and, about 800 B.C., the Dorset culture, which spread from its core area in northern Hudson Bay and Foxe Basin, to northern Ellesmere Island, west to Victoria Island and south to Newfoundland. For the incredible span of nearly 2,000 years, while civilizations emerged and decayed in other lands, the Dorset people held sway in a nearly unvarying pattern of life in most of the North American Arctic.

Their culture was distinctly Eskimoan. They probably invented that emblem of Inuit ingenuity, the igloo. They used — and may have invented — the kayak, probably the most efficient and certainly one of the most beautiful hunting boats ever designed by man. They knew the toggle harpoon, but they probably did not use sled dogs and pulled their small, ivory-shod sleds themselves.

The Inuit still remember them. They call them *tunit*, a long-ago race of gentle giants, preternaturally powerful but rather stupid. "They were so strong," Labrador Inuit told the anthropologist E.W. Hawkes in 1914, "that one of them could hold a walrus (weighing more than a ton) as easily as an Eskimo a seal (weighing about 150 pounds)." Yet strangely enough, the Dorset, pictured as dumb giants in most tales, seem to have been an intensely mystic people. They produced perhaps the most beautiful art of the Arctic: exquisite figurines of falcons, ptarmigans, bears and humans. Most of this art probably had religio-magic significance and may have been used in shamanistic rituals. These tiny masterpieces of ivory, bone or antler once held the hopes and fears of this long-vanished race.

The Inuit's cold-adapted hunting culture reached a state of near perfection with the arrival of the so-called Thule culture people, direct ancestors of today's Inuit, who moved eastward from Alaska about A.D. 800. Within less than 200 years, they had spread across most of the North American Arctic, displacing or absorbing the Dorset people.

Superb sea mammal hunters, Thule culture Inuit pursued and killed everything from the small ringed seal to the giant bowhead whale. They invented, perfected and passed on to the Inuit of historic times such a plethora of specialized tools and hunting

*A Polar Inuk in northwest
Greenland hunts seals by kayak.*

equipment that J.A. Ford of the American Museum of Natural History described them as "gadget burdened." This is the more amazing because not only was their land exceedingly cold, hostile and barren, but it was also poor in those raw materials most societies have found essential. Metal was rare: only brittle, hard-to-work meteoric iron and native copper were found in a few places. Driftwood was abundant in some areas, and rare to nonexistent along most arctic coasts. That left stone, ice, snow and sod as the most readily available materials that the land and sea provided. Equally vital to the Inuit were the materials they obtained from the animals they killed: bone, horn, baleen, antlers, teeth, ivory, furs, skins, sinews and intestinal tissues. As Dionyse Settle, the chronicler of explorer Martin Frobisher's second expedition to Baffin Island, so shrewdly observed in 1577: "Those beastes, flesh, fishes, and fowles, which they kil, they are meate, drinke, apparel, houses, bedding, hose, shooes, thred, saile for their boates ... and almost all their riches."

They had superb skin-covered boats, the large spacious umiak, which could carry a dozen people plus a cargo of a ton or more, and the sleek fast kayak, which Frobisher's men admired: "they rowe therein with one ore, more swiftly a great deale, than we in our boates can doe with twentie."

They were efficient hunters, but like all predators they had to live in balance with their prey. Studies show that the population of the southeast coast of Baffin Island was about 100 to 150 people 4,000 years ago (Pre-Dorset); 100 to 150 people at the time of Christ (Dorset); 150 to 200 people when Queen Elizabeth I ruled in faraway England (Thule); 250 in 1952 when Queen Elizabeth II became their sovereign; and 286 in 1984.

Small groups of humans in the immensity of the Arctic, superbly adapted to the demands of their realm, whether as hunters or herders, the people of the north lived in a world apart. They knew nothing of the southern world, and for millenniums southern man knew nothing of them.

ARCTIC WATERS

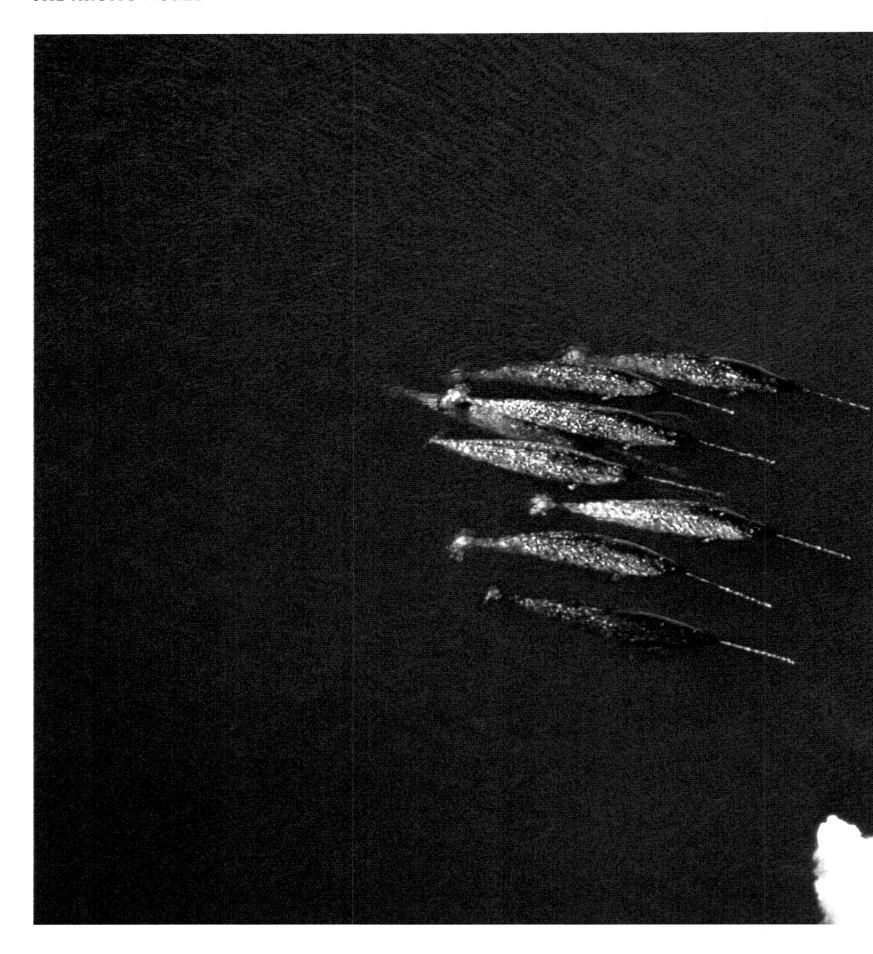

ABOVE *Horned puffins* (Fratercula corniculata) *in their summer plumage. The puffin's large beak enables it to catch and hold several fish at one time.*

LEFT *Only the male narwhals* (Monodon monoceros) *have these spiraled ivory tusks, which can be up to ten feet long.*

OVERLEAF *Great 600-pound northern fur seal* (Callorhinus ursinus) *bulls keep close watch over their "harems" of much smaller (60 to 100 pound) females.*

ABOVE *Young male Steller sea lions* (Eumetopias jubata) *wrestle upon a wave-washed rock. The massive adult bulls of this species can weigh more than a ton.*

LEFT *Of all arctic ducks, the male king eider* (Somateria spectabilis) *is the most resplendent. The female is a modest brown. She usually nests near tundra ponds and lakes.*

OPPOSITE *Calved from the huge glaciers of northwest Greenland, this iceberg near the north Labrador coast of Canada has been polished and shaped by wind and water during its thousand-mile journey.*

TOP *Harp seal* (Pagophilus groenlandicus) *mother and pup. Harp seals spend summer and fall in the Arctic. They migrate south in winter.*

ABOVE *Parakeet auklets* (Cyclor-rhynchus psittacula) *are seldom seen on land except when nesting.*

LEFT *A polar bear crosses the smooth ice of a tundra pond in late fall.*

ABOVE *A pod of belugas* (Delphinapterus leucas), *the gregarious white whales of the north.*

LEFT *A black guillemot (*Cepphus grylle) *carries a fish to its young.*

OPPOSITE *Black-legged kittiwakes.*

OVERLEAF *An island off Greenland.*

CHAPTER 5

Early Exploration

THE NEED TO ADAPT to cold and changing climatic conditions may have made early man inventive and ingenious. But warmth and agriculture gave him leisure to contemplate his world, and from time to time civilized southern man glanced toward the north with a shiver of fear and fascination. "The whole of the country," stated the Greek historian Herodotus about 430 B.C., "has so hard and severe a winter that there prevails there for eight months an altogether unsupportable cold."

They imagined it as a frore and fearsome land, and only one man in antiquity is known to have visited it. Pytheas was an eminent astronomer and geographer in the Greek colony of Massalia (today's Marseille). About 330 B.C. he sailed into the Atlantic, up the coasts of Iberia and France, circumnavigated Britain, reached the Orkneys and other islands so far north that "the sun rose again a short time after it had set," and sailed northward from there to a land to which he gave an immortal name: *Thule*, the *Ultima Thule* of the Romans, the utmost bound of the earth. It may have been Iceland or northern Norway. The sea there was covered by a strange substance so that "it can neither be traversed on foot nor by boat," which may have been brash ice or pack ice, and just beyond Thule, the sea was "congealed," *mare concretum*, as Pliny later put it so graphically.

It was a brief and tantalizing glimpse into an alien, forbidding world. With Pytheas, arctic exploration begins, and also ends for many centuries. The Romans were overland empire builders; they marched a lot but rarely sailed, and never to the north.

While the north remained remote and fabled, a few of its products were greatly desired and highly priced in the south: amber, ivory and exotic animals. Ptolemy II, king of Egypt (285 – 246 B.C.), kept a polar bear at his private zoo in Alexandria.

Romans pitted polar bears against seals in "aquatic battles" staged in flooded arenas. And Japanese court annals report that in A.D. 858 the emperor received two polar bears as a gift. By what strange routes live polar bears reached the south, the records unfortunately do not tell.

The "amber road" is better known: from the shores of the eastern Baltic Sea up the Vistula, across the Alps to the centers of civilization. Baltic amber has been found in the tombs of several pharaohs, and amber was common, though costly, in Rome.

The ivory routes were much more complex. They reached north through Eurasia to many places along the Arctic Ocean, with perhaps a branch line across Bering Strait into North America, and funneled the north's ivory wealth to Turkey, Egypt, Iran and China, the countries where it was in greatest demand. The ivory came from three animals: the extinct mammoth; the narwhal, the small arctic whale whose male has a single, spiraled tusk up to ten feet long; and from the walrus. Since only the tusks of these disparate animals reached the south, descriptions of their original owners ranged from fanciful to fabulous. The mammoth, which provided China with much of its ivory for more than 2,000 years, was known as *yin shu*, "the hidden rodent," for it was thought to be an underground beast that died upon exposure to light. Walruses were believed to be giant, tusked fish and narwhals, unicorns.

These ancient trade routes brought ivory, polar bears and "unicorn horns" to southern markets. But with them came little knowledge about the north, because it was in the interest of traders to keep their sources secret. One who did report in detail about his northern travels was Ottar, the Norse chieftain who visited England's King Alfred the Great. One day, he told the king, "he fell into a fantasie and desire" to know the utmost north. About A.D. 890 he sailed along Norway's coast, rounded North Cape (Europe's northernmost point) and the Kola Peninsula, and sailed southward into Russia's White Sea. The entire coast, he said, was "a wildernesse and desert country" sparsely settled by "a few fishers, fowlers, and hunters, which were all Fynnes [Lapps]."

Apart from adventure and curiosity, Ottar made the trip to hunt "horse-whales" [walruses], which have teeth "of great price and excellencie ... Their skinnes are also very good to make cables for shippes ... " (A thousand years later, A.E. Nordenskjöld passed the same area and noted that among its main products were " ... walrus tusks and lines of walrus hide." Anthropologist F.G. Rainey has called walrus thong "the strongest line known before the invention of the steel cable.")

In medieval times, polar bear skins were worth a fortune, and captive polar bears were prized by kings.

Ottar's chief wealth consisted of tribute he exacted from the Lapps: marten skins, baleen, barrels of eiderdown, bear rugs, and thong made of walrus and seal skins. Being "discovered" could have its drawbacks for the long-isolated people of the north. By 1557, a contemporary account notes, the Lapps were paying taxes "to the Emperour of Russia, to the King of Denmarke, and to the King of Sweden."

Tribute and trade from the Asian Arctic flowed mainly toward Mongol-ruled China. Marco Polo concluded the account of his long (1271–1295) sojourn in Kublai Khan's realm with a brief description of the north: a "Region of Darkness," where "during most of the winter the sun is invisible," inhabited by "bears of a white color, and of prodigious size" and by people who traveled on sleds pulled by dogs. The Tartars, noted Marco Polo, "often go on plundering expeditions against these people," which does explain the northward drift of some Siberian tribes.

The Arctic's wealth was furs and falcons: the finest furs in the world and the largest and most magnificent of all falcons, the white gyr, the bird of kings and emperors. They came, said Polo, from an island in the "Northern Ocean" where vast numbers were captured "and carried to various parts of the world." Most went to Kublai's court, for the khan liked to travel in style "attended by full ten thousand falconers, who carry ... gerfalcons, peregrine falcons, and sakers ..."

In the east, the call of the Arctic was trade and pillage. In the west, at first, it was a monkish search for peace and solitude, and for the *Insulae Fortunatae*, the "Islands Of The Blest," a place of heavenly delight believed to be somewhere in the western seas. St. Brendan, called "the Navigator," was born in about A.D. 484 in Ireland's County Kerry, founded several monasteries and traveled widely. When he was 70, the story goes, he set out with 17 other monks to visit the Blessed Isles. They built a large curragh, its frame of ash laths "covered with oak-tanned oxhides and caulked with ox-tallow." The Irish curragh, like the umiak, the walrus-skin-covered boat of the Inuit which it resembles, was an extremely strong and seaworthy craft. In it they sailed north and west, reaching, some scientists think, North America.

The story of St. Brendan's voyage is a typical imram, an Irish tale full of marvels and fancy, and spiced with a few intriguing facts. They sailed to the "Island of Sheep," no doubt the Faeroes, whose name means "Sheep Islands" in Old Norse; discovered the "Paradise of Birds," which could be any of the seabird colonies of that region; and reached the "Island of Fire," probably volcanic Iceland. To St. Brendan, too, we owe a first and wonderful description of an iceberg, "a crystal mountain in the sea." He measured it and said it was 1,400 cubits (2,000 feet) high, but even saints exaggerate.

Finally, far to the west, shrouded in fog, they found the Islands Of The Blest. And that, some say, was Newfoundland. The fog fits, all else is conjecture. It could be done. In 1976, historian Timothy Severin and a crew of four sailed a curragh, built exactly like the one used by St. Brendan, from Ireland to Newfoundland. And recently, upon a lichen-covered boulder in northern Newfoundland, some incised lines were found that resemble ogham, an early Irish script.

Although Brendan's voyage is problematic, Irish monks did settle in uninhabited Iceland, far from women and temptation. By A.D. 800 about 1,000 of these long-haired anchorites lived in peace beneath a midnight sun so bright, reported Dicuil, a learned Celt at the court of Charlemagne in A.D. 825, that the monks could "pick lice"out of their shirts as easily at midnight as at noon.

ABOVE *Ivory-tusked male narwhal. In medieval Europe, the tusks were worth more than their weight in gold.*

RIGHT *Walruses upon an island off Alaska.*

Walrus bulls packed close together at a favorite hauling-out place. Their ivory tusks have been in great demand for at least 2,000 years.

Their peace was rudely shattered by the arrival about A.D. 860 of a very different people, the Norsemen. Brawny, brave and brawling, they were a rough lot but, according to naval historian S.E. Morison, at that time and for centuries to come "the most expert navigators of the western world." In the south, these fierce warriors in sleek dragon ships pillaged and sacked the coastal cities. To Iceland they came as settlers, because good farmland was then already scarce in Norway.

Among the latecomers who arrived in Iceland were Thorvald and his teenage son Eirik, known as "the Red," for he had red hair and a fiery temper. He and his father had to leave their native Norway because of "some killings," as a saga laconically reports. After some years in Iceland, Eirik was involved in another feud, and he was banished for three years. Following reports of land to the west, he reached Greenland's ice-girt east coast, sailed south around Cape Farewell and traveled up west Greenland's deeply indented shores. It was an empty land.

They found "traces of people who had lived there, and bits of skin boats and stone implements ..." but the people, Dorset culture Inuit, had vanished.

Climate favored the Norsemen. It had been cold from about A.D. 300 to 700. Then it warmed, reaching a climatic optimum which lasted from about A.D. 900 until 1200, bad for the seal-hunting Dorset who died out or moved north, but good for prospective Norse settlers and their livestock. Like a shrewd real estate promoter, Eirik called the ice-capped new land "Greenland," for "men would be drawn to go there if the land had an attractive name."

He returned to Greenland in A.D. 986, leading a flotilla of 25 ships filled with colonists, their cattle and their chattel. Some perished in a storm, a few turned back, but 14 ships with about 400 settlers made it and sailed into the spectacular, meadow-flanked fiords. There they built homes of stone, sod and roof timbers taken along from Iceland, because Greenland had no trees.

Other settlers followed, and in time their farms were concentrated in two areas: the "Eastern Settlement" in the present Julianehaab district and, farther north, the "Western Settlement" in the Godthaab (now Nuuk) region. In about 1100, when the colony was at its peak, it had 300 farms, 16 churches, a cathedral, a monastery, a nunnery and altogether about 3,000 people who, in this remote outpost, continued to lead a modified version of contemporary north European life.

They were subsistence farmers. They kept sheep and as many of the tough, scrawny cattle as their range could support. They made butter and cheese, spun wool and supplemented farm food with game and fish. They maintained a lifeline to Europe for some essential goods and a few luxuries: grain, iron, timber, some clothes, plus wine and beer, and such trinkets as they could afford.

To pay for the imports, they exported three items of immense value: live polar bears, then worth in Europe the equivalent of a ship plus cargo, and polar bear skins; gyrfalcons, for which European and Arab rulers paid fortunes; and narwhal tusks, marketed in Europe as wonder-working "unicorn horns," which were worth several times their weight in gold. And they paid their tithes to the papal see and special levies in support of Holy Land crusades in walrus ivory.

To obtain these arctic treasures, the most daring settlers made *Nordrsetur* trips to a region with "many glaciers and seals and white bears." Since the average temperature at that time was about 7 °F warmer than it is now, and ice cover consequently less extensive than at present, they may well have sailed and

The gyrfalcon (Falco rusticolus) *was the most valuable of all falcons, prized equally by the Holy Roman Emperors and the great khans of Asia.*

rowed far north into Melville Bay. In these northern regions, they sometimes met a people they contemptuously called *Skraelings*, "troll-like barbarians." "They had large eyes and broad cheeks," say the sagas, and "possess no iron, but use walrus tusk for missiles and sharpened stones instead of knives." Inuit and Norsemen may have fought, and they probably occasionally traded. In recent years, archeologists have found Norse goods in prehistoric Inuit houses on Ellesmere Island: pieces of chain mail, some woolen cloth and Inuk-made figurines of long-faced, narrow-nosed Norsemen.

In the summer of 1001, the Norsemen also traveled west and south. Leif the Lucky, Eirik's son, and a crew of 35 sailed toward land seen earlier by an off-course, Greenland-bound ship. They first came to an icy land with sloping rock beaches and called it *Helluland* ("Flat Stone Land"), probably Baffin Island. Sailing south they reached densely wooded Labrador and called it *Markland* ("Forest Land"). Still farther south, they came to a lovely land where the vines hung heavy with grapes, and Leif called it *Vinland* ("Wineland"), perhaps because it was true, but probably just to promote the place. It is nearly certain that Vinland was at the north tip of Newfoundland where, at L'Anse aux Meadows, the Norwegian scientists Helge and Anne Stine Ingstad discovered the remains of a Norse settlement. Leif and his crew built houses of wood and turf, spent the winter, and returned the following summer in triumph to Greenland, their ship laden with valuable Markland timber.

Other Norsemen went to Vinland; the expedition led by the Icelander Thorfinn Karlsefni consisted of 3 ships, 250 settlers, their wives and "all kind of livestock." But this was not an empty land. The Norse occasionally traded but more often fought with the resident Skraelings (either Dorset Inuit or ancestors to Newfoundland's now extinct Beothuk Indians), who vastly outnumbered them. They finally had to abandon this farthest outpost, a saga says, "on account of those who already inhabited the land."

In Greenland, too, the Norsemen were in dire trouble. After 1200 the climate became much colder, and as the ice moved south, so did the ice-loving seals and the seal-loving Inuit. The Black Death in Europe, wars and growing piracy disrupted their tenuous bond to the "Old Country." With increased cold, their marginal agriculture declined. The people, skeletons reveal, were undernourished, weak, rachitic. The cold-adapted Inuit encroached. The Norsemen's gallant effort petered out. When the Renaissance Pope Alexander VI expressed concern in 1492 for his Greenland flock "situated at the end of the world," the last had died, as Byron said, "unknell'd, uncoffin'd and unknown."

A young peregrine falcon (Falco peregrinus).

Their ship crushed by ice, members of Willem Barents' 1596 expedition built a driftwood house and spent the winter in it.

CHAPTER 6

The Arctic Route to Cathay

WHILE IN FARAWAY GREENLAND the last Norsemen died, a new spirit enlivened Europe. The somber, plague-ravaged Middle Ages — gloomy, mystic and introspective — gave way to the exuberant Renaissance — brilliant, daring and rich. The Portuguese explored Africa with its ivory wealth, rounded the Cape of Good Hope and reached India in 1497, breaking the Arab stranglehold on European trade with the Orient. Christopher Columbus, bound westward for India, found America, and Ferdinand Magellan, also in Spain's service, circumnavigated the world, stopping at the Moluccas, the fabled Spice Islands.

The immensely profitable trade with the glamorous east was now a Spanish-Portuguese monopoly, to the intense chagrin of other maritime nations, especially England and Holland. Barred from the southern routes to "the world of golde, precious stones, balmes, [and] spices," they hoped to find one in the north, and thus began the nearly obsessive, centuries-long search for a Northeast or Northwest Passage. The Arctic was not a goal, but merely a monstrous but surely not insuperable obstacle on the northern road to Cathay.

Patrons and explorers, dazzled by visions of fame and fortune, readily believed the widespread fallacy that a northern route would be easy. Wrote the eminent Flemish geographer Gerardus Mercator in 1580: "The Voyage to Cathaio by the East, is doubtlesse very easie and short ..." Sir Humphrey Gilbert, who later claimed Newfoundland for England, advocated the northwest as the ideal "Passage to Cataia," because, he said, it was short, easy and would belong exclusively to England. And the London merchant Robert Thorne wrote to King Henry VIII in 1527 and offered a third and even simpler route: up to the Pole and then downward "to what part [of the world] they list."

This was another delusion, firmly believed by some scientists and explorers until the end of the 19th century, that beyond a narrow northern belt of ice there lay an open polar sea.

And thus, lured by hope and lulled by ignorance, began the European exploration of the north. The arctic reality, they quickly found, was, as the poet Milton said so aptly:

> Mountains of ice, that stop the imagined way
> Beyond Petsora eastward to the rich Cathaian coast.

But the Elizabethan sailors and their successors were a doughty lot and not easily discouraged. They poked and probed, north, east and west, in tiny ships, grimly determined. Cathay eluded them, but incidental to the search, they explored and crudely mapped much of the north, and brought back detailed information about the northern lands, their wildlife and their people (as well as a few unfortunate natives taken along, in the fashion of the time, as curios and samples). They also laid the basis for two immensely important companies: the Muscovy Company, which brought Russia and its fur wealth within the ken and trade of western Europe, and the still-flourishing Hudson's Bay Company, which spread across North America and now has stores in most towns and villages of the Canadian north. And they discovered the whale wealth of the Arctic, which led, over centuries, to the near-extermination of bowhead whales, and to the decimation of arctic populations through contact with whalers and their diseases to which the natives had little or no immunity.

John Cabot and Jacques Cartier tried it first and discovered Newfoundland and Canada, poor China substitutes, but worth a lot in fish and furs. Having "failed" in the west, Cabot's son Sebastian organized a major expedition via the east, led by Sir Hugh Willoughby and Richard Chancellor. Assuming that the trip would be easy, they were advised to be "innocent as doves, yet wilie as serpents" once they reached China.

They sailed in 1553. Willoughby's ships got stuck in ice off Lapland, and he and all his men froze to death. Chancellor reached Russia's White Sea, traveled by sled to Moscow and was graciously received by Ivan IV. The tsar favored trade, the Muscovy Company was chartered in 1555, and English ships sailed regularly to the White Sea to load the goods their Moscow agents had collected: wax, flax, tallow, cables of hemp and walrus hide, and "trayne oyle," the oil of white whales, seals and walruses. Above all, they came for furs, though London counseled discretion: "sables bee not every mans money, therefore you may send the fewer" but of "marterns, minivers [ermine] and Mynkes ... you may send us plentie ... "

Others pushed farther east. Stephen Burrough, Chancellor's second-in-command, and his servant Richard Johnson set out in 1556 in the pinnace *Searchthrift* to try and reach the river Ob, of which they had heard rumors. They met the Nenets (Samoyeds) and reached "Nova Zembla, which is a great lande … and there wee saw white Foxes and white Beares." Ice caught them and held them, and they spent the winter on the arctic shore together with the natives. Johnson attended a shamanistic séance and was immensely impressed when, as a grand finale, the shaman took a long sword, warmed it over a fire "and thrust it through his bodie … *in at his navill and out at his fundament …*" They bought walrus ivory and polar bear skins, but they did not reach the Ob.

Foiled in the east, the English tried the west. In 1576, Martin Frobisher sailed northwest into the unknown, reached Baffin Island and met people that "bee like to Tartars." Relations were poor. The Inuit kidnaped five of his crew, and Frobisher, an immensely powerful man, snatched an Inuk plus kayak out of the water and took him back to England. He also picked up a glittering stone, which an assayer pronounced to be high-grade gold ore.

And that made the Arctic interesting. In the south, the Spaniards were hauling shiploads of gold out of their American possessions, which pained Queen Elizabeth I. A second expedition was quickly organized. Upon the 25-acre "Countesse of Warwicke Islande," which the Inuit called *Kodlunarn*, the "White Man's Island," at the entrance to Frobisher Bay, they found "good store of Ore, which in the washing helde golde plainly to be seene." Gold fever gripped them, and from Frobisher down, all men, "both better and worse," dug feverishly. They amassed 200 tons and sailed jubilantly for England.

The ore, experts said, was excellent. They made a cost analysis and estimated that each ton of ore contained £7.15s worth of gold and £16 of silver. Transport from Baffin Island cost £8 per ton and refining £10 per ton, leaving a profit of more than £5 per ton of ore shipped from the Arctic. Heartened by such splendid news, venture capital poured in, and in 1578 Frobisher led a fleet of 15 ships to the Arctic with orders to mine 2,000 tons of ore, to build a fort and to leave a "settlement" of 120 men. Fortunately for them, the ship carrying the prefabricated house sank, and that part of the plan had to be abandoned.

Thirteen ships reached Kodlunarn Island and, while from nearby cliffs Inuit watched in amazement, Elizabethan sailors and miners dug the deep trenches still there today. They even tried agriculture in this barren, icy land and "sowed pease, corne and other graine, to proue the fruitfulnesse of the soyle against the next yeare." But there was to be no next year. When the adventurers returned with their hoard, they were told that further analysis had proven the ore to be worthless. All that glitter had been mica. After that costly fiasco, arctic mining was out of favor for more than 300 years.

Their gold fever doused, England's merchants returned to their original tack. They sent the noted mariner John Davis to find the Northwest Passage. He tried three times, in 1585, 1586 and 1587, rediscovered east Greenland, sailed up the west Greenland coast, crossed Davis Strait, explored Baffin Island's Cumberland Sound, sailed south, noticed Hudson Strait but did not enter, and explored the coast of Labrador.

Although the northern land held little attraction, Davis was, like Frobisher, awed by the wealth of the northern sea. Frobisher met the now nearly extinct bowhead whales in large schools, as if "they had bene Porposes." Davis also saw "great store of Whales," and off west Greenland he ran into harp seal herds in "marveilous great abundance." Except in Labrador, where two of his men were killed, Davis usually had good relations with the Inuit. He bartered iron for meat and fish, and the sailors wrestled with the Inuit and were amazed at their strength and skill. Although he did not find the Northwest Passage, he wrote undaunted to a backer: "The passage is most probable, the execution easie … "

This was precisely what worried the Dutch. What if their busy English rivals found the passage first? Backed by the States General and private interests, Willem Barents sailed in 1594 far north to Novaya Zemlya and into an open Kara Sea. Instead of pushing on, he returned with this joyous news to Holland. Fortune favored him only once. The next year the Kara Sea was, as usual, blocked by ice. He tried again in 1596, steered far north and discovered and named Bear Island and Spitsbergen (Svalbard). His ship was crushed by ice near the coast of Novaya Zemlya. They built a stout house of driftwood logs and spent the winter, full of fear and suffering, beleaguered by hungry polar bears. Barents and some of his men died. The others, traveling in small, open boats reached Lapland the following summer. At this time the Dutch reached the East Indies via the south, and lost all interest in putative northern passages.

Not so the stubborn English. In 1607, the Muscovy Company asked Henry Hudson to sail to Cathay via the North Pole. Ice stopped him at 81° N near Spitsbergen, but he returned with reports of great numbers of bowhead whales, "which whale," the Muscovy Company happily noted, "is the best of all sorts." There were 30 tons of blubber on a large bowhead, and 4 tons of it rendered into 3 tons of valuable oil. From the roof of its

94

ABOVE *An 18th-century artist's etching of Martin Frobisher on one of his expeditions to the Canadian north.*

RIGHT *Spitsbergen (Svalbard).*

cavernous mouth hung 600 to 800 baleen plates, 10 to 13 feet long, the "sieve" with which whales strain masses of small crustaceans from the arctic sea. In the days before plastics, baleen had many uses, most importantly as the "whalebone" in women's stays and corsets. So valuable was baleen that at one time a single bowhead whale could pay for a two-year whaling voyage. No wonder that the English, and then the Dutch, Germans and French, rushed north to capture whales. Soon 500 to 600 ships sailed north each year. The Dutch built Smeerenburg (Blubbertown) at the northwest tip of Spitsbergen. There, at nearly 80° N, they had taverns, a church, bakeries and a bordello.

Between 1675 and 1721, the Dutch alone employed 5,886 ships and took 32,907 whales with a gross value of $82,267,000. As the whales became scarce, arctic whalers, at first mainly Dutch, then British and finally predominantly American, swept all arctic seas for their valuable prey until, when the hunt ceased in 1913, bowhead whales were nearly extinct.

Hudson, whose report started whaling in the north, then had another try at the Northwest Passage. In 1610, he sailed through Hudson Strait into Hudson Bay and south along its eastern shore. After a long winter of cold and suffering, his crew had but one thought: to provision their ships at the Digges Island murre colony and sail for home. When Hudson insisted that the search for a passage to Cathay continue, most of the crew mutinied, and he and six others were left behind in an open boat.

As a strait leading to China, Hudson Bay was a failure. But the English soon found another use for it. In the south, the French were making fortunes out of Canada's immense fur wealth. By building forts on James and Hudson bays, the English hoped to reroute this lucrative trade to the north and themselves. And thus, in 1670 was born the "Company of Adventurers of England Trading Into Hudson's Bay," better known as the Hudson's Bay Company, to which King Charles II, with matchless magnanimity, granted 1,486,500 square miles of land, nearly half of the future Canada. One of the charter's provisions enjoined the company to seek a Northwest Passage. This it ignored, since it might lure rivals into its domain. Instead it spread, first along the coasts of James and Hudson bays and then inland. It merged with its great rival, the North West Company, and kept expanding westward until it collided with another gigantic fur empire, that of Russia, advancing from the east.

FROM THE
MOUNTAINS
TO THE SEA

ABOVE *A valley on Attu, the westernmost island of the 1,000-mile-long Aleutian chain. A moist climate accounts for the lush growth.*

OPPOSITE *Although they appear to be static masses of ice, glaciers advance or retreat as the snow around them accumulates or thaws.*

OVERLEAF *The mountains of the Taymyr Peninsula in eastern Siberia.*

ABOVE *Caribou crossing the mud flats of the Horton River, Northwest Territories.*

OPPOSITE, ABOVE *Pure-white ivory gulls* (Pagophila eburnea) *breed on a nunatak, an ice-surrounded mountain in the farthest north on Ellesmere Island.*

OPPOSITE, BELOW *A freighter on the Lena River in Siberia.*

ABOVE *"Flagged" trees near the tree-line in subarctic Canada. At the treeline, the boreal forest ends and the treeless tundra begins.*

RIGHT *A carpet of caribou moss* (Cladonia rangifera), *which is really an immensely abundant lichen, covers the floor of the boreal forest. It is a main winter food of caribou and, in Eurasia, of reindeer.*

ABOVE *A sea of rocks, Repulse Bay area, Northwest Territories.*

RIGHT *The midnight sun in Swedish Lapland. During the summer months in the Arctic, the sun shines 24 hours a day.*

OPPOSITE *Spring breakup in the Brooks Range.*

TOP *The advancing and receding ice sheets of the last ice ages carved the rugged, deeply indented coast of Labrador.*

ABOVE *Ibyuk, the tallest pingo in the world, near Tuktoyaktuk in the Northwest Territories. An earth-covered mountain of ice created by permafrost action, this pingo is 157 feet high, nearly 1 mile around at its base and at least 1,000 years old.*

LEFT *A polar bear at nightfall on the newly formed ice of Hudson Bay.*

ABOVE *Their kayaks tied in tandem, Polar Inuit haul a killed narwhal to their camp on the shore of Inglefield Bay in northwest Greenland.*

OPPOSITE *The Mackenzie River delta, Northwest Territories, is a maze of channels and islands stretching down to the Beaufort Sea.*

OVERLEAF *The Vilyuy River in the central Siberian taiga, early fall.*

CHAPTER 7

Fur Empires of Siberia and Alaska

WHEN RICHARD CHANCELLOR, after his vain attempt to find a Northeast Passage in 1553, met Ivan IV, one of the tsar's many titles was "Commander of all Siberia, and of the North parts" — most impressive, except for one detail: the tsar did not as yet own any part of Siberia. Moscow, in fact, had only recently broken the shackles of Mongol rule. Yet in less than a century, in her quest for furs, she would span a continent, reach far into North America and create one of the greatest empires of all time.

Kiev, far to the south, had been the head and heart of Russia until the Mongol armies sacked and destroyed it and most other Russian cities (1237–1240). Only the northern city-state of Novgorod was spared. Its wealth was trade. For centuries it had been the mart where northern goods were exchanged for those of western Europe, brought in by Norse and later Hanseatic merchants. Slowly Novgorod's might spread north and east. By 1200, she obtained in trade and tribute from tribes along the arctic coast walrus ivory and cables made of walrus hide, white whale hides, whale oil, gyrfalcons, and furs, above all furs, the "soft gold" of the north. It was an ancient trade. Writing of the "Rus," the early Russians, the Arab geographer and traveler Ibn Rustah noted in A.D. 912 that "Their only business is to trade in sable and squirrelskins and other kinds of skin … " Furs were immensely valuable and important.

Its population swelled by refugees from the Mongol scourge, Moscow expanded, slowly at first and then with explosive speed and energy. It absorbed neighboring principalities and in 1471 defeated Novgorod, taking over its vast possessions and trade connections in the north. Moscow became Russia and Ivan IV its first crowned tsar. In 1555, he established trade with

LEFT AND BELOW *Fur seals (Callorhinus ursinus) on Alaska's Pribilof Islands, discovered by the Russian explorer and fur hunter Gerasim Pribilof in 1786.*

*A male fur seal (*RIGHT*) sniffs one of the females of his harem. Once severely decimated, the fur seals on Alaska's and Siberia's islands are nearly as numerous now as centuries ago.*

England's Muscovy Company. In the east and south his troops conquered the major Tartar khanates of Kazan (1552) and Astrakhan (1556). But when he reached toward the Baltic Sea, he was defeated by Sweden and Poland. Foiled in the west, his southern flank secured, the tsar looked eastward toward fur-rich *Sib-ir* — "the sleeping land." Rather than conquer it himself, he leased it for 20 years to the Stroganovs. To obtain it was their problem.

The Stroganovs had early hitched their fortunes to Moscow's rising star and were the wealthiest family in Russia, with holdings that stretched to the Urals. They were the Astors of the Russian north. To conquer Siberia they engaged Cossacks, freemen and freebooters from the Don, and as their leader, Yermak, a ruthless man, whose previous occupation had been to plunder Volga shipping. In 1581, Yermak and 840 followers breached the Ural Mountains and defeated Kuchum, khan of Sib-ir, the main town of Siberia, near today's Tobolsk. Two years later, Yermak drowned and the advance was temporarily checked. But then it swept on, with Russian troops, often spearheaded by Cossacks. In 1641, they reached the Sea of Okhotsk. In 60 years this tiny band of men, never more than 2,000, had spanned a continent for furs and conquered a land 25 times the size of France.

The vastness of the enterprise and the seeming ease of its success were due to several factors. The many tribes of Siberia, Marco Polo had already noted in the 13th century, were "not united under the government of a king or prince." Once Kuchum fell, because his forces had no firearms, all organized resistance ceased. The incentive to conquest was the eternal dream of wealth, of endless furs from untapped forests, for already in the 16th century the most valuable furbearers were becoming rare in European Russia. In 1581, when Yermak set out for Siberia, a single sable skin was worth the equivalent of a 50-acre farm. Eighty years later, Kamchatka natives traded eight sable skins for a knife and sixteen for an axe.

In many ways Siberia resembled Canada when the Europeans came: natives that were poorly armed and quickly cowed, hostile to the invaders yet keen to trade with them, and a sparsely populated land rich in furbearing animals. In the late 17th century New France sent 500,000 beaver skins annually to Europe. In 1590, Moscow demanded, but did not necessarily get, a yearly *yasak* ("tribute") of 200,000 sable skins, 10,000 black fox skins and 500,000 squirrel skins.

Furs were wealth. By 1650, nearly one-third of Russia's total income was derived from furs. Politically, furs could buy favors or secure friendships. In 1595, Tsar Feodor Ivanovich sent a gift of 400,000 pelts to the Holy Roman Emperor. Furs were a vital export, for Russia had developed an expensive habit. In 1638, the Mongol ruler Altyn Khan sent the tsar a gift of furs and ten *poods* (328 pounds) of *chai*, and soon all Russia, from tsar to peasant, was hooked. Tea became the national drink and furs were needed to pay for it. Fortunately the Chinese, who had the tea, were crazy about furs. Traders met at Kyakhta, a border town, and by 1750 this trade, primarily in furs, was worth four million rubles to the Russians, more than $100 million dollars now.

The people who produced Russia's fur wealth were the natives of the north, and from the beginning of the Siberian conquest and through later years, the tsars insisted that they be gently squeezed. The economic enslavement of natives began. Fridtjof Nansen wrote angrily in 1893 about the "Russian traders, who barter with the natives, giving them brandy in exchange of bearskins, sealskins, and other valuables, and who, when once they have a hold on a man, keep him in such a state of dependence that he can scarcely call his soul his own." Corruption was widespread and conditions were often chaotic. Travel was slow and difficult. In winter it was so cold, exhaled breath froze instantly with a dry, crackling sound called "the whispering of the stars" by poetic Siberians. A message from Moscow might take a year or two to reach its destination.

In 1648, Semyon Dezhnev — Cossack, adventurer and *yasak* collector — traveled with 90 men in 6 *kochas*, primitive flat-bottomed boats, down the Kolyma River to the Arctic Ocean. (From the far north came the most valuable sable, thick-furred, silky and nearly black.) He sailed along the coast, around the east tip of Asia (now called Mys Dezhneva), through the strait later named after Bering, and into the Gulf of Anadyr. It was a historic trip of utmost importance, for it proved that Asia and America were separate continents, divided by a strait, and not linked as was then widely thought. But none knew of this achievement, because it took 87 years for Dezhnev's report to reach Moscow. All that time it lay unnoticed and unread in a Yakutsk archive.

Throughout most of his long reign (1682–1725), Tsar Peter I tried to turn his nation west. During the last weeks of his life he looked east, toward Asia, to his vast, shadowy realm beyond the Urals. The dying tsar wrote a last, terse order: proceed to Kamchatka; build two ships; ascertain whether Asia and America are linked; make maps and return. To lead the expedition, he selected Vitus Bering, a Dane who had long served in Russia's navy, a diligent but plodding man who had no love for science.

An old engraving of Bering's ships, the St. Peter *and* St. Paul, *in the harbor at Petropavlovsk on the Kamchatka Peninsula, 1740.*

It took three years to reach Kamchatka and build the ships. Everything from nails, to ropes, to anchors had to be transported 6,800 miles from St. Petersburg to the Pacific coast by horse-drawn sleds, by river boats and by dog teams. After this enormous effort, the expedition itself was brief and inconclusive. Bering left in July 1728, groped through the northern fog, found St. Lawrence Island (now part of Alaska), passed blindly through the fog-shrouded passage already discovered by Dezhnev and later named Bering Strait by James Cook, reached 67° N and, fearing winter and satisfied in his own mind that America and Asia must be separate continents, returned in six weeks.

St. Petersburg was not impressed, but was willing to give him a second chance. Plans multiplied and received imperial favor and funds. Academicians advanced pet projects and had them approved. At last it grew into the Great Northern Expedition with a sweeping mandate: to explore all Siberia. It was the most ambitious, prolonged and grandiose northern expedition ever undertaken and, considering the times, the means then available, and the distances and obstacles to be surmounted, perhaps the most successful, though at a high price in suffering and sacrifice. Foremost among its many objectives was to find the American coast and map it from the far north to Mexico, and that at a time when New York was just a Dutch hamlet in a little-known land.

Drawings of a fur seal, a sea lion and a sea cow from the chart of the St. Peter's voyage, 1741.

The logistics were staggering. More than 900 men took part in the expedition. Mountains of *matériel* had to be moved across Siberia. Bering was 51 when he left St. Petersburg. He was 60 when he arrived on the Pacific coast to undertake his main task, to find America.

He and his second-in-command, Aleksey Chirikov, sailed in the ships *St. Peter* and *St. Paul* in June 1741. Fog and storms soon separated the vessels. Bering continued east and on July 16 he saw in the distance the snow-glittering peaks of the St. Elias range. He had reached the goal of his 16-year search: *Al-ey-as-ka*, "the great land," as the Aleuts called it. But Bering was tired and discouraged, sapped, perhaps, by incipient scurvy. He stopped at Kayak Island only long enough to take on fresh water. Georg Wilhelm Steller, the brilliant young biologist aboard his ship, rushed ashore, collected 160 species of plants, many new to science, and that night noted bitterly in his diary that after all these years of preparation and suffering, they had come merely to take American water back to Asia.

The return trip was terrible. They were pounded by storms and finally ran aground on an island, later called Bering, one of the then unknown Commander Islands east of Kamchatka. They built primitive shelters of turf, driftwood and ship's timber on the icy, treeless island. Steller had watched Kamchatka natives dig up roots and corms of various plants, as food and antiscorbutic. Now he did the same, but the sailors would have none of it. Bering died of scurvy and so did many of his crew. The island was aswarm with arctic foxes. They ate everything, stole everything, they chewed on the dead, and they bit the dying. The scurvy-crippled sailors hated them: they burned them, skinned them alive, mutilated them, partly gutted them, blinded them. It was a horrid winter.

Only Steller, the scientist, was healthy, busy and endlessly fascinated. There was the Steller's sea cow, never seen or described before, so easy to kill that, discovered in 1741, it was extinct by 1768. There was the elegant spectacled cormorant that would soon share the sea cow's fate. There were great herds of sea otters, then tame and trusting, staring at the sailors with curious old-men's faces. And in spring the fur seal legions came to breed on ancestral beaches, where the dark rocks were worn smooth by their millennial coming and going.

The survivors built a boat from the wrecked *St. Peter* and reached Kamchatka. With them they carried 900 sea otter pelts. When Siberia's *promyshlenniki*, the fur hunters, saw those, their eyes glittered with greed. Sable was superb, but sea otter fur was the densest, warmest, most luxurious fur in the world. The Chinese gladly paid 100 rubles a pelt at a time when most people were lucky to earn that much in a year.

There were no ships on the Pacific coast, so the *promyshlenniki* built *shitiks*, vessels made of green lumber, the planks sewn together with thong or osier withes and caulked with moss. With such ships they set out into a sea which, according to the U.S. Coast Pilot, has "the most unpredictable [weather] in the world. Winds of up to 90 miles an hour are commonplace ... and howling storms may be expected at any time during the year." One ship in three did not return.

The *promyshlenniki* ignored such odds. They were a breed of northern conquistador, and here the gold was furs. They robbed and enslaved the Aleuts and sent cargo after cargo of sea otter pelts back to Siberia. Imperial *ukases* thundered against "such barbarities, plunder, and ravaging of women." It did not help. St. Petersburg was half a world away. The *promyshlenniki* killed many. Introduced diseases took most of the rest. In a few decades, the Aleuts had been reduced from an estimated 16,000 – 20,000 to barely 2,000.

Life in Siberia was becoming settled. Irkutsk already had 16,000 inhabitants. Ten thousand post horses at 75 stations assured rapid transport from Siberia to Moscow or St. Petersburg. But at the far frontier of Alaska it was a chaotic free-for-all. Although admonishing her subjects to treat "their new brethren [the Aleuts] ... with greatest kindness," Empress Catherine II, a believer in *laissez-faire*, was not about to intervene. "It is for traders to traffic where they please. I will furnish no men, ships, or money," she declared. And so it was at first not the state, but a rich Irkutsk merchant, Grigori Shelekhov, who took over Alaska. He arrived off Kodiak Island with two ships in 1784, blasted the local, warlike Koniags with cannon just to let them know who was boss, then treated them kindly and paid them

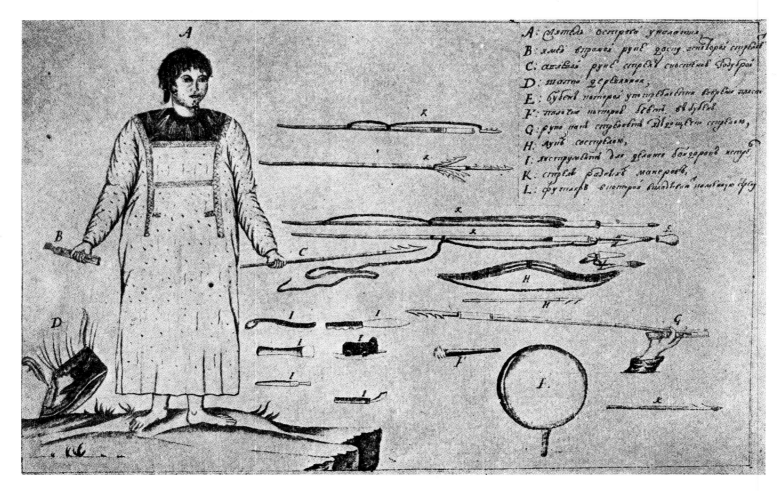

An old drawing of an Aleut from Alaska.

for helping to build his fort and village at Three Saints Bay. His colony established, Shelekhov rushed to St. Petersburg to lobby for a trade monopoly and money. He got neither, and for several years the colony teetered on the edge of extinction.

It might have died, had not Tsar Paul I approved in 1799 the formation of a monopolistic and truly imperial enterprise, the Russian-American Company, with wealthy shareholders, vast privileges and headquarters in St. Petersburg. Equally important was that Aleksandr Baranov, who managed Alaska for the company, was a true empire builder: tough, shrewd and totally honest. Known as the "Lord of Alaska," he shipped 30 million rubles worth of furs to Russia. Yet after 27 years of service, he died a poor man.

He built forts and settlements. He defeated the warlike Tlingit Indians. He tried to keep the encroaching British, American and Spanish, all eager for sea otter pelts, out of his dominion, or he made shrewd deals with them. To feed his struggling colony, he built in 1812 Fort Ross in California, 62 miles north of Spanish San Francisco, and manned it with a few Russians and many Aleuts. It never was the hoped-for success. The Aleuts were splendid hunters, but hopeless as farmers. Fort Ross could barely feed itself.

The main problem for Baranov and his successors was the clash between the two gigantic fur companies, the Russian-American and the Hudson's Bay Company. They fought bitterly along the poorly defined border, inciting various tribes to raid rival company posts. A mutually advantageous peace was arranged when the two great governors of the north finally met, Sir George Simpson, the "Little Emperor" of the Hudson's Bay Company, and the famous explorer and governor of Alaska, Baron Ferdinand von Wrangel. Simpson offered to provision Alaska from the Hudson's Bay Company farms in Oregon, and Wrangel promised to market a portion of Alaska's fur through the H.B.C. Fort Ross, now no longer needed, was sold in 1841.

Alaska was always more colony than part of Russia. Under Baranov about 500 Russians lived in Alaska, and about 1,000 under Wrangel. But there were too many clerks and clerics, and not enough settlers. It was a transient, mainly male population, which lived by trading furs. However, sea otters were declining rapidly. Between 1742 and 1911, when the few survivors received protection, about a million sea otters were killed in Alaska. Such odd but lucrative enterprises as selling 20,000 tons of Alaskan lake ice at $35 a ton to cool the drinks of sweltering Californians could not make up for dwindling fur sales.

Above all, in Alaska Russia was overextended and vulnerable. It was 9,300 miles from St. Petersburg to Sitka, Alaska's capital. Foreign traders and raiders went nearly everywhere at will. In 1822, a Russian expedition to Alaska's far-northern region found that traders, both Russian and American, had preceded them, taking out furs and leaving guns and syphilis. America encroached from the south, England by sea and overland from the east. Finally, reluctantly, judging the risks and costs too high, and the profits, if any, too low, Russia decided to sell, and in 1867 the United States acquired Alaska for $7,200,000. Two years later, the Russian-American Company's arch-rival, the Hudson's Bay Company, was forced to sell its realm to newborn Canada for £300,000. Nations acquired the northern empires founded on furs.

The 1849–1850 British naval expedition to the Arctic in H.M.S. North Star explored parts of northwest Greenland and wintered in Wolstenholme Sound, Greenland. Four crewmen died of scurvy.

CHAPTER 8

Arctic Knights

MUTINEERS WERE USUALLY HANGED. Yet Henry Hudson's rebellious crew escaped scot-free when they returned to England in 1611, having left their captain and his loyal men to die in new-found Hudson Bay. They were spared because it was fervently hoped that they had the key to unlock the Northwest Passage to the infinite riches of Cathay.

England's wealthy businessmen immediately formed the "Governor and Company of Merchants of London, Discoverers of the Northwest Passage." They financed several mutineer-guided expeditions into the inland sea, and only grudgingly accepted the fact that it was a bay and not a passage. In 1616 they sent the master mariners Robert Bylot (Hudson's erstwhile mate) and William Baffin toward the north to find the Northwest Passage, where John Davis had searched for it in vain a generation earlier.

Bylot, Baffin and a crew of 15 sailed the *Discovery*, Hudson's old ship, up the west coast of Greenland. They rarely landed because "the wether was so exceedingly foule," but they did meet Inuit in the Upernavik region and traded metal objects for narwhal tusks. Cautiously and skillfully, Baffin weaved the small vessel through the pack ice and emerged on July 1 at 75°10' in the North Water, the greatest polynia of the Arctic, larger than Switzerland in summer, about one-tenth that size in winter, always free of ice and one of the great sea mammal havens of the north. This great open sea "anew revived our hope of a passage." They circled Baffin Bay, reached Smith Sound in the farthest north (named after Sir Thomas Smith, an important backer and member of the Muscovy Company), poked into ice-choked Jones Sound (named after Sir Francis Jones, Lord Mayor of London), failed to realize that Lancaster Sound was the entrance to the longed-for passage, and returned to England. There is no passage, Baffin reported, only an immense number of whales, all "easie to be strooke, because they are not used to be chased ..."

It was an amazing voyage and it marked the end of an era: of valiant captains in small ships sailing north into unknown seas, their doomed but daring quests financed by "merchant adventurers." Priorities changed. Baffin, who had made five extensive trips to the Arctic, died in 1622 on Hormoz Island in the still-vital Strait of Hormuz between Oman and Iran, where the combined forces of England and Shah Abbas I of Persia routed the Portuguese who controlled the southern routes to the east. The Arctic had not repaid exploration and lapsed again into icy obscurity. Until 1818, world maps carried a rough outline of Baffin Bay with the remark "according to W. Baffin, 1616, but not now believed."

The Hudson's Bay Company and later its rival the North West Company (they merged in 1821) were, as Washington Irving said, "Lords of the Lakes and Forests" in a large part of North America. The Company ruled its vast realm with just though often severe paternalism, and made and maintained peace among hostile tribes, since the natives' endless internecine wars were bad for business. It opened new trading posts and new territories wherever furs and profits beckoned. The Arctic, found costly and unrewarding, was rarely visited. Exploration by others was discouraged.

The Russians, after their Cossack-led sweep from the Urals to the Pacific and beyond it into Alaska, settled down to digest the largest empire on earth. It was a period of pacification and consolidation. Strife among native groups was suppressed. Settlers arrived, some voluntarily, others not. The torch of scientific curiosity brought to Siberia by Tsar Peter's savants sputtered and died in the hands of bureaucrats and traders. The Arctic interested them only insofar as it provided furs.

The Dutch were the master whalers of the 17th and 18th centuries, as well as far-ranging, aggressive traders. Near Spitsbergen the once vast whale populations had been nearly exterminated by the 1630s, and the whaling fleet moved to the "West Ice," the enormous crescent of pack ice between Spitsbergen and Greenland. In 1719, two adventurous Dutchmen eased their tubby, high-pooped whaling vessels around Greenland's Cape Farewell and sailed up its west coast into Davis Strait. All along the edge of the shifting pack, huge bowhead whales lolled in the water — a promise of wealth. Four years later, 350 ships, mainly Dutch, German and Basque, were hunting whales in Davis Strait. The Dutch augmented profits by trading with the

Icebergs continue to be a problem for ships in the northern seas.

Greenland natives, paying for furs, oil and baleen with cloth, metal objects and, often, with *genever*, cheap but potent Dutch gin. Occasionally they kidnapped natives and sold them to menageries and fairs in Europe. So notoriously ruthless were these whaler-traders, the Dutch States General felt compelled to pass an act in 1727 forbidding the "robbery and murder of the native populations."

Missionaries occasionally preceded and often followed the traders (the H.B.C. initials of the Hudson's Bay Company were ironically interpreted as "Here Before Christ"), and they left a lasting religious as well as cultural imprint upon the natives of the north.

The Danes regarded themselves as the legitimate heirs of Greenland's vanished Norsemen and, partly to forestall the Dutch, launched in 1721 a combined missionary-trading venture to Greenland, led by the Lutheran pastor Hans Egede. The "Apostle of Greenland," like most of his successors and compeers, was a man utterly devoted to his task and to his chosen flock, but with that stern Savonarola righteousness that rarely understands the failings of less driven and devoted people. He saw it as his duty to lead the natives "out of their blasphemous and bestial state," and spent an often frustrated lifetime imbuing the easy-going, individualistic Inuit with the dour Protestant ethic of his time. While Egede and his followers changed the spiritual, moral and, to some extent, social life of the Inuit, they were careful, after some disastrous failures, not to interfere with their traditional hunting-fishing life, which provided the trade goods so vital to the missions' survival. Out of Egede's precepts evolved the benevolent paternalism that marked Danish rule in Greenland during the next two centuries.

The Labrador coast, Newfoundland governor Sir Hugh Palliser reported to the British government in 1766, "is inhabited by the most savage people in the world — the Eskimos." They had ample reason to be savage. Encroaching European fishermen had already exterminated the Inuit along the north shore of the Gulf of St. Lawrence and now threatened the roughly 3,000 Labrador Inuit. The odds were against the natives. In 1766, 1,500 European vessels caught fish off the south Labrador coast.

At this critical juncture, German Moravian Brethren offered to establish missions on the Labrador coast. They demanded, and got, 100,000 acres to go with each mission, as a sort of *cordon sanitaire* to keep the corrupting influence of the fishermen away from their imperiled flock. They founded Nain in 1771, and other mission settlements in quick succession.

At all of the missions, a brother opened a vellum-bound diary each night and wrote in meticulous Gothic script about the

125

day's events: of hopes and hardships and loneliness, of men and women who meant well yet found it hard to understand the people they had come to serve and teach. The missionaries forbade the "heathen" dance and song festivals, and one early convert quit with the words "I stop believing in Jesus and will have a good time." Another, who had many wives, refused to give them up, explaining "he needed them to row his boat."

In this century, Brethren from England took over the missions, but echoes of the Germans' long service persist: many Labrador Inuit own musical instruments and play Bach, Mozart and Brahms; and they count in German, use German-derived names for weekdays, and many have German names.

The Aleuts have Russian names and have adopted so many Russian words into their language that I can follow the gist of a simple conversation. They (and some Alaskan Inuit and Indians) adhere to the Russian Orthodox faith. Services are held in Church Slavonic, the ancient liturgical language of Slavic Orthodox churches, which nearly all adult Aleuts can speak, a legacy of Russia's priests who brought their version of Christianity to this, the remotest corner of the Russian realm. Today, these people are strangely tri-cultural: the core is Aleut, wrapped in a many-faceted layer of Russian custom and belief, the whole covered by an American patina.

The 19th century also worshiped other gods: science, nation, progress, knowledge. Scientific aspirations rather than mercantile goals now launched arctic expeditions. It was an age of conquest — the conquest of nature by man. Arctic explorers set forth like Arthurian knights upon a gallant quest, with firm faith in their ships, their science and their inherent superiority. Natives, usually called "savages," were viewed either with contempt or as romantic, arctic curiosities. The fact that their very existence proved that they knew how to live in the Arctic did not impress itself upon the explorers. To learn from such barbaric people was simply out of the question.

The explorers paid for their illusions with terrible suffering and bore it, as a rule, with heroic fortitude. Many were raised in Britain's navy and were molded by its beliefs, discipline and traditions. The miracle is that so few men, encumbered by the prejudices and the ignorance of their time, explored so much of the Arctic.

In 1817, at the urging of Sir Joseph Banks, president of the prestigious Royal Society, Britain's Admiralty decided to resume the search for the Northwest Passage. With the end of the Napoleonic wars, it had ships and men to spare, and was eager to serve science and add to Britain's national prestige. Captain John Ross and Lieutenant William Parry sailed on June 17, 1818,

On William Parry's 1819 expedition, the crews of H.M.S. Hecla *and* Griper *cut into Winter Harbour, September 26.*

in H.M.S. *Isabella* and *Alexander*.

North of Greenland's Disko Bay, Ross came upon 45 whalers huddled near the edge of the "Middle Pack," a broad belt of pack ice between Greenland and Baffin Island. Ross and Parry rammed their ships through the pack. The whalers followed and emerged in the wake of the explorers in the whale-rich North Water. Ross continued north. On August 8, as he made his ships fast to the floe edge in northern Melville Bay, he spotted men upon the ice. The Polar Inuit had been discovered.

A thousand years ago, during a relatively mild climatic period, Inuit lived as far north as there is land. Around 1200, the climate began to deteriorate. It was the beginning of the Little Ice Age, which lasted, with intermissions, until the 1850s. The ice cover of the arctic seas increased, whales began to avoid these ice-choked waters, and the Inuit of the farthest north moved southward or died out. Only one small group remained, the Polar Inuit of northwest Greenland, living at the edge of the North Water in a region exceptionally rich in game. As the centuries passed, the memory of other people faded into legend, and the 200-odd Polar Inuit believed they were the only people on earth in a land bordered by eternal ice. The appearance of Ross' ships naturally filled them with terror. They mistook the

ABOVE *On one of Sir John Franklin's overland expeditions (1821), after making their way to the sea from Great Slave Lake, the expedition members used canoes to explore the arctic coast.*

LEFT *Winter quarters on Somerset Island of Sir John Ross' second expedition, 1832–1833.*

sails for wings and thought the ships were gigantic, magic birds come from space to kill them.

To lure them closer, Ross asked John Sacheuse, his South Greenland interpreter, to put presents on the ice. He had come well prepared. His supply of gifts for natives of the Arctic included 200 mirrors, 102 pounds of snuff, 129 gallons of gin and 40 umbrellas. Once Sacheuse had established some rapport with the astounded, fur-clad natives, Ross and his officers, in full-dress naval uniforms, walked across the ice to meet them. "Do you come from the moon?" the Inuit asked.

Their initial dread allayed, some visited the ships and "their astonishment was unbounded." Here there was mystery and wealth beyond the wildest dreams of mortals, and they reacted to it with a touching mixture of awe and avarice. For people living in a land where the only metal was meteoric iron, brittle and hard to work, and where even a small piece of driftwood constituted a treasure, the ship was a sort of floating Fort Knox, and they admired everything and then tried to carry it off.

Ross sailed on, verified Baffin's observations made two centuries earlier and, like Baffin, failed to realize that Lancaster Sound was the long-sought-for entrance to the Northwest Passage. But he had shown whalers the way to the north, and soon 40 to 100 ships sailed to the North Water each year with such regularity the Polar Inuit called them *upernagdlit*, "the bringers of spring."

As in other regions of the Arctic, the whalers also brought more deadly gifts, diseases to which the long-isolated natives had no immunity. In 1830, 12 years after Ross, whalers discovered a camp of corpses near Cape York. In another 30 years, more than half the Polar Inuit had perished.

The British Admiralty, though disappointed that the Northwest Passage had not been found, was elated with the general success of Ross' expedition and promptly planned the next one. To the Victorian era, the Arctic was what the moon and space are to ours. Arctic travel, like space travel, yielded much scientific information but no immediate financial benefits. It conferred prestige upon participating nations and brought fame to many explorers. It was risky, it was romantic, and the public loved it, sharing vicariously in the thrills and hardships by reading all about it in newspaper accounts, or in the spate of books that followed expeditions. Arctic explorers first rushed home, and then rushed into print.

The naval expeditions, like space explorers, went north as self-contained units. The ships were their homes, and they were provisioned for two to five years. Officers hunted, but mainly as "sport," shooting ptarmigan and waterfowl, but rarely seals that would have provided large quantities of fresh meat.

Parry, Ross' second-in-command, led the next expedition in 1819, and fortune favored him. It was an exceptionally ice-free year, and he sailed west through Lancaster Sound and Barrow Strait all the way to Melville Island, where he spent the winter. In subsequent years, he probed into other sounds and inlets, and tried to find a passage through northern Hudson Bay. He also attempted to reach the North Pole, the second Holy Grail of arctic exploration, by sailing to Spitsbergen and then hauling heavily loaded boats and sleds across the ice toward the Pole, against the slow but steady drift of Arctic Ocean ice. It was like climbing a treadmill; as they labored north, the ice carried them south. Once, in four days of terrible toil, they advanced one mile.

The polar knights, John Ross, his nephew, James Clark Ross, Parry, Frederick Beechey and many others, persisted. They approached from the west via Bering Strait and from the east through Hudson Strait or Lancaster Sound. They came overland, aided by a somewhat reluctant Hudson's Bay Company, sailed down the great arctic rivers and explored the arctic coasts. Slowly the vast white spaces on northern maps were filled with the outline of islands, separated by a labyrinth of channels, inlets and sounds.

They mapped the Arctic; they collected its plants and animals; they lugged home tons of rocks and fossils; and they described its quaint inhabitants. But they did not really understand the place, and finally disaster struck. In 1845, Sir John Franklin, a veteran explorer, set out with 2 ships and 128 officers and men to conquer the Northwest Passage. Their ships were caught and held by heavy ice in Victoria Strait, between King William and Victoria islands. Survivors struggled toward the mainland, hauling heavy boats on heavy sleds, loaded with some useful items and many useless ones, such as dinner plates and silver cutlery. It was a march of the doomed; all died of exhaustion, starvation and scurvy.

In death, Franklin became perhaps the most famous of all arctic explorers. About 40 expeditions were sent north to search for him. Although they failed in their primary purpose, to find Franklin and his men, their cumulative effort unlocked much of the Arctic.

Methods changed. John Rae of the Hudson's Bay Company, the first to find traces of the Franklin expedition, traveled with small boats, lived largely by hunting and, after shivering through one winter in a stone house he had built, spent his second winter in a "much warmer" igloo. The last of the great arctic explorers — Robert Peary, Vilhjalmur Stefansson, Knud

Sailing up the coast of Greenland in search of the Northwest Passage.

Rasmussen, Otto Sverdrup and others — combined Inuit methods and experience with southern technology and knowledge. They dressed in the superbly warm fur clothing made by Inuit women, traveled with dog teams, knew how to live off land and sea animals, and were often assisted by native guides and helpers.

While the explorers probed ever farther into the last unknown reaches of the Arctic, its romantic appeal and its wildlife lured a very different breed to the north, men of position and wealth. Prince Napoleon, nephew of the emperor, sailed in 1856 aboard the corvette *La Reine Hortense* to the lonely island of Jan Mayen. As the ship skirted the pack ice, the prince and his entourage sat down to a "sumptuous banquet" served in an elegant salon while an orchestra played "selections from the best operas." Few traveled in such splendor, but many took their yachts to the north, to see the sights and to rapture about it at home.

The "sportsmen" hunted. As one of them, J. Russel-Jeaffreson, reported in the latter part of the 19th century, "The accessible hunting-fields of the world are now getting played out, yearly more sportsmen turn their faces towards the Arctic, where good hunting may be obtained." Some took their yachts. Others hired Norwegian sealing vessels at £500 to £800 for

ABOVE *Crew aboard the whaling ship* Maud, *1889.*

LEFT *Blacklead Island whaling station, Canada, September 1903.*

Whaleboats sailing through the ice off the west coast of Southampton Island, Canada, June 1904.

the season and went to east or west Greenland, Spitsbergen, Novaya Zemlya and even into the Kara Sea and, as the poet Longfellow put it so aptly:

> There we hunt the walrus, the narwhal, and the seal.
> Aha! 't was a noble game.

More plebeian, less comfortable and infinitely more deadly than the wealthy dilettanti were the professional whalers, walrus hunters and sealers. Having hunted the great bowhead to the brink of extinction in most regions of the north, the whalers invaded its remotest haunts, the Chukchi and the Beaufort seas. The rarer the whales, the more valuable they became. By 1900 an average bowhead was worth $10,000 and a large one up to $15,000, and that at a time when in the United States factory workers earned a dollar a day. By 1914, of a once-great circumpolar multitude, less than 1,000 bowhead whales were left.

While Norwegian hunters in small sloops killed the remaining walrus herds at Spitsbergen, in the Kara Sea, near Novaya Zemlya and the recently discovered Franz Josef Islands, American whalers and walrus hunters shot them in the Bering and Chukchi seas, more than 200,000 between 1860 and 1880 alone. By 1914, of an estimated 300,000 walruses, about 40,000 survived.

The sealers killed millions of harp and hooded seals, as well as thousands of polar bears, north of Russia, and east of Greenland and Canada, a highly controversial hunt that continues to this day.

Wherever the whalers touched, the native people perished. Within one generation, 50 percent of Alaska's coastal Inuit were dead. In 1888, when the whalers came to the Beaufort Sea, more than 1,000 Mackenzie Inuit inhabited the region. Twenty years later, less than 100 were left. With the whales gone, the whalers went. They left a land and a sea despoiled and a native people decimated and racked by disease.

The explorers, too, began to lose interest in the Arctic. The great goals had been attained. The Swede A.E. Nordenskjöld sailed through the Northeast Passage (1878–1879). The Norwegian Roald Amundsen conquered the Northwest Passage (1903–1906). Fridtjof Nansen set his ship, the famous *Fram*, into the arctic ice and drifted with it across a large portion of the Arctic Ocean (1893–1896). In 1909, Robert Peary reached the North Pole. With that the Arctic, having ceded its secrets and bereft of much of its former wildlife wealth, lost most of its appeal to both explorers and exploiters.

*Inuit sisters in the central Canadian
Arctic play with a favorite doll.*

CHAPTER 9

From Furs to Factories

THE 1920s AND 1930s were a quiet time in the north, the lull before the hurricane of change that would sweep away a millennial way of life. Canada's north was "ruled" by a very conservative trinity: Royal Canadian Mounted Police, missionaries and merchants, all dedicated to the status quo. The natives lived in small camps scattered across the north and came to trading posts and missions only a few times a year, to trade, to pray, to visit and gossip, or to help unload the annual supply ship, usually the sole link with the "outside" world.

Greenland slumbered in Denmark's kindly embrace. Here, too, the natives lived, as they had always done, in small camps or villages along the coast. It was official policy to keep corrupting outside influences away from the natives, and since the state controlled trade and the trading ships, Greenland's isolation was fairly easily maintained.

After the wild exuberance and chaos of the Nome (1898) and other gold rushes, when the white population soared briefly from 4,000 to more than 30,000, most left again, and Alaska lapsed once more into obscurity, perceived by the south as a remote, romantic hinterland of little value or importance. Moose browsed in the willow thickets where the apartment blocks of Anchorage now stand.

The great changes came earlier to Siberia but not to its arctic regions. Construction of the Trans-Siberian Railroad began in 1892. It was built across difficult terrain at a rate of 370 miles a year and was completed in 1905. Industry came to Siberia. Mines and factories were opened. The population, four million before the railroad, quickly doubled. In the 1920s and 1930s the development of Siberia accelerated. But even then, the far north remained relatively untouched, unchanged.

The Arctic's time had not yet come. Cryolite, used as a flux in aluminum smelting, was mined in southwest Greenland from 1856, and in 1906 John Longyear of Boston began coal production on Spitsbergen where, since the end of the Little Ice Age in the 1850s, the possible shipping season had increased from three months to about five months. But these were mere pinpricks in a vast region. The northern seas had been heavily exploited. The northern lands remained untouched.

World War II clearly showed the strategic importance of the north. Planes were ferried to England via the Canadian north, Greenland and Iceland. Germany established weather stations on Spitsbergen and east Greenland. In June 1942, Japanese forces occupied Attu and Kiska in the Aleutians, U.S. soldiers built the 1,523-mile Alaska Highway between March and September 1942, and by mid-1943, more than 140,000 American (and some Canadian) troops were stationed in Alaska. In later years, chains of D.E.W. (Distant Early Warning) line stations spanned the North American north, and similar chains, no doubt, were built in the Soviet Arctic.

In 1951, the Polar Inuit of northwest Greenland were still very isolated, their only brief contact with the outside world the visit of the annual supply ship. That summer an armada of ships arrived at North Star Bay. The Americans had come to build the giant Thule Air Base. To the 302 Polar Inuit, it was part miracle, part nightmare. Within months, they were joined by thousands of American servicemen. Some Inuit who had gone north in spring to hunt found, upon their return in late fall, a full-fledged military town on the broad, flat peninsula they used to call *Pitufiq*, "the place where one leaves boats."

The Arctic rushed, with only a brief transition, from stone age into space age, from a culture that had adapted to arctic conditions to another able to conquer the Arctic with its advanced technology and to transfer southern conditions to the north. Ekalun, an Inuk with whom I lived for many months at a remote camp in the Canadian Arctic, was about ten years old when he and his people were "discovered" by members of the Stefansson-Anderson expedition. In his youth he led a hunting life similar in many ways to the life of Europe's ice age hunters 20,000 years ago. Now he had several guns, and a large canoe and outboard motor. He listened to news in Inuktitut on his battery-operated, made-in-Japan radio, and carried a Swiss-made watch. But we still lived year-round in tents, dressed in fur clothing, slept on fur-covered sleeping platforms, and ate nearly exclusively meat and fat of the animals the Inuit hunted.

That was in 1969 and now seems infinitely strange and remote. Most Inuit in Canada today live in two- and three-

Kenipitu Inuit women in formal dress, Fullerton, Northwest Territories, c. 1903.

bedroom houses and many, in the larger settlements, live in apartment buildings. Few have seen an igloo, and fewer still would know how to build one. Snowmobiles have replaced dog teams, and big boats with outboard motors are the rule; only in a few Alaskan villages are umiaks still used, and kayaks only in Greenland. Most Inuit have government jobs or work for industry, though many still hunt on weekends and during holidays.

With stunning rapidity, the Inuit have acquired the blessings of southern civilization: the material comforts and rewards that money can buy, security and freedom from famine, good medical services and schools. But they have also inherited the curses of southern life. Cardiac disease, formerly unknown among the active, rarely worried Inuit, is now a common killer of harried urban natives. Cancer, rare in former days when they ate primarily meat and fat, afflicts an ever-increasing number of arctic people. Their changed diet has had other detrimental effects. Once famous for their perfect teeth, the Inuit have now,

A fishing trawler passes split fish hung to dry upon a rack in arctic Norway.

according to a report by the World Health Organization, the worst tooth decay of any people in the world. The screaming, roaring snowmobiles are literally deafening; hearing loss among natives is extensive.

Alcohol and drug abuse are the scourges of the north. In Greenland one in ten deaths is alcohol related. In Canada's Northwest Territories, the leading causes of death for native peoples are violence, suicide, accidents and poisoning, most of them connected with alcohol abuse.

Gradually, though, a new awareness has come to the north of a heritage shared by all northern people. And, based on this past, the people try to build another life, a synthesis of old and new, of north and south, of northern values and traditions supplemented and enhanced by southern knowledge and technology. Hopes diverge and may be difficult to reconcile. People dream of a pristine Arctic with ample wildlife to sustain their traditional life as hunters and trappers. Yet they are dazzled by the vast mineral resources their arctic realm possesses, and dream of the great wealth that will flow their way when these are exploited.

On his way to the Arctic in 1908, along the Athabasca River, Vilhjalmur Stefansson noticed tar "which here and there trickled down the cut-banks of the river." Natural gas flared in the wilderness. To Stefansson it was "the torch of Science lighting the way to civilization and economic development to the realms of the unknown North." The Alberta tar sands are expected to yield 500,000 barrels of oil daily by 1987. Diamond Jenness, anthropologist on Stefansson's last expedition (1913–1918), heard from natives on the Alaska coast about a "strange lake of 'pitch' ... which poisoned any bird or animal that drank from it." Now an 800-mile pipeline carries oil from this region to the ice-free port of Valdez in southern Alaska, and supertankers take it from there to the south.

In February 1968, the Atlantic Richfield Oil Company struck oil near Prudhoe Bay on Alaska's North Slope, and further drilling proved the existence of an immense oil field. The companies concerned planned the pipeline to take the oil to the southern markets, applied for permits to build it and, with the magisterial assurance of industrial giants, ordered the pipe from Japan. And then the unthinkable happened. The companies' right to build the pipeline was challenged in court by Alaska natives and by conservation groups. The natives felt that if the mineral wealth of their ancestral land was to be sold south, they should have some say in the matter and receive a healthy slice of the financial pie.

Conservationists maintained that the pipeline and its load of

An Inuit mother and child shopping for groceries.

oil could lead to widespread ecological disasters, and that, if this or any other pipeline was to be built in the north, its construction should be preceded by thorough research and carried out with the most painstaking adherence to environmental guidelines. It was the dawn of environmental awareness, oil still flowed cheaply and abundantly from the Middle East, and the case dragged on for years. Pipeline construction finally began in 1975. The pipeline and oil terminal at Valdez cost nearly $10 billion, about eight times the originally estimated cost. Complying with stringent environmental protection rules, which proved to be very expensive, were part of the cost.

It was a test case and, in a way, all parties won. The natives won the Alaska Native Claims Settlement of 1971, which gave the state's 85,000 aboriginal people 68,726 square miles of land (roughly 12 percent of Alaska) and nearly $1 billion in cash. Environmentalists proved that even the mightiest of industrial juggernauts could be stopped and made to pay more than lip service to environmental concerns. And industry got its pipeline and its oil, albeit at a much higher cost than anticipated. (In the meantime, though, oil prices had risen steeply and profits were, after all, most gratifying.)

Since then, the stakes have soared. Alaska now has proven reserves of 7 billion barrels of oil and 32 trillion cubic feet of

A seal, food for his family, is brought to the floe edge by a kayak hunter in northwest Greenland and hauled to firmer ice by his son.

natural gas. It may have additional recoverable reserves of up to 38 billion barrels of oil and 171 trillion cubic feet of natural gas. The oil and gas reserves in the Canadian north may be as large or larger. And they, in turn, are surpassed by the giant reservoirs of oil and natural gas found in the Soviet north. In addition to gas and oil, there are in the north some of the largest deposits on earth of coal, iron, copper, lead, zinc, asbestos, wolfram, uranium, gold, diamonds, phosphates and rare metals. Except for Quebec's $15 billion James Bay hydroelectric system and a few giant systems in Siberia, the north's hydropower potential has barely been touched. The Arctic is like a unique and magnificent crystal palace crammed with the most marvelous treasure. The trick will be to get the treasure out without destroying the palace.

The north is the last great wilderness region on earth and home to half a million natives, many still hunters and herders,

Inuit hunters in Frobisher Bay with a large bearded seal they have shot from their motorboat.

whose distinctive, nature-linked culture and tradition must have wilderness and space and wildlife, or it will wither and die. The north is a sensitive, unforgiving land, quick to hurt and slow to heal. Tracks left in the high Arctic by the hand-drawn carts of early explorers are still visible after 160 years. Crude oil will slowly degrade and vanish in warm seas. In cold seas it takes 50 times longer to degrade and may not vanish for decades or even centuries. Mistakes made in the north will haunt us through many generations. Not surprisingly, the four principals — industry, government, environmentalists and natives — have differing, often conflicting and occasionally shifting visions of the north.

Industry wants to get the northern treasures to southern markets wherever and whenever it is profitable to do so. Since there is no such thing as a corporate conscience, industry's environmental concerns are in direct proportion to government, public and native pressures. In a moment of candor the senior executive of an arctic exploration company said: "We're not really all that interested in the scenery and the animals. What we want to do is to make some money out of it." And yet, industry has spent hundreds of millions of dollars on arctic impact studies and, when forced to and the need for the resource

OPPOSITE AND ABOVE *The impact of southern technology on the Arctic's native peoples, its wildlife and the land has been immense.*

is high, can be very cautious and careful, passing additional costs on to the public.

Governments would like to make everyone happy and, since this is impossible, react to current pressures, needs and the public's real or imagined concerns. Government looks with favor upon industry for it provides employment and taxes. Government also responds, as best it can, to the public will, but it is never quite sure which public to respond to: the large southern public which consumes the northern resources yet emotionally demands that the romantic Arctic be preserved intact, or to the northern populations, numerically small but very vocal and emotional, and guided by excellent (often government-funded) lawyers. The loudest, best-reported lobby often wins, at least temporarily, to the detriment of long-range goals and policies.

Twenty-five years ago some environmentalists pleaded that the entire north be kept inviolate and quoted hopefully the philosopher Henry David Thoreau's dictum that "in wildness is the preservation of the world." It was a wonderfully clear-cut, emotional appeal. Unfortunately, it was also totally unrealistic. Now they accept the need for some development, but insist it be done with the least possible damage, and they try to curb the creeping blight of poorly regulated exploitation.

Environmentalists also stress that the north's value is not solely in mineral deposits. At present rates of consumption, the vast reserves of arctic oil and gas will be gone in one generation. The mineral wealth is finite. The north's magnificence and mystique are eternal unless they are now destroyed. The call of the wild is strong upon urban man. Each year more tourists visit the north. A few years ago, scientist Dr. Fred Roots said that "It is entirely possible the value to the country of the open space will exceed the value of the minerals in the polar region."

The natives, understandably, would like to have their cake and eat it too. Wilderness is the base of their hunting culture; this "old way of life," as it is now usually called, and this inimical land continue to exert a tremendous emotional allure for northern people. A young Inuk, Adamie Angiyou from Povungnituk on the east coast of Hudson Bay, has put it well: "We are changing, but the pull of the land is still very strong on us. There is much hardship to being on the land, but we do not feel it when we are there because we are free." Some Inuit have left the relative comforts, and the social problems, of the settlements and towns and have returned to the land. There is a great desire for independence, yet a continued dependence upon the south, its goods and its wealth. When Greenland achieved home rule in 1979, Queen Margrethe II told its 50,000 people, "You now hold the future in your own hands." But

143

90 percent of the money needed to maintain Greenland's standard of living comes as a subsidy from Denmark.

The problems and aspirations of the "new North" are endless, the solutions are difficult now and will be more difficult in the future. The south and its technology push relentlessly north into the land of hunters and herders. Visitors fly casually to the North Pole. Polar bears equipped with radio collars are tracked by satellite. By the year 2000, it is expected that great fleets of L.N.G. (liquefied natural gas) tankers will ply the Northwest Passage summer and winter. In the future, there may be climatized cities in the Arctic, shielded from the environment by geodesic domes. Great northern rivers will be rerouted toward the south, to supply it with clean water, to raise the level of the shrinking Caspian Sea, to irrigate the deserts. Attempts will be made to change the climate of the north (for the better, planners hope) by building, for instance, a dam across Bering Strait, or by melting the ice of the northern seas with concentrated solar power beamed upon earth from a space station. The Arctic of the world, so ancient and unchanging, is changing now at an overwhelming speed and is rushing, like all of us, toward an uncertain future.

And yet, there is only
One great thing,
The only thing:
To live;
To see in huts and on journeys
The great day that dawns,
And the light that fills the world.

Inuit poem recorded by Knud Rasmussen

POLAR ANIMALS
AND BIRDS

ABOVE *A flock of ravens (*Corvus corax*) flies up from the bank of the Mackenzie River, where they had been feeding on dead fish washed ashore. Incredibly hardy, the circumpolar raven lives as far north as there is land.*

ABOVE, LEFT *Ptarmigan* (Lagopus) *change their plumage to match the colors of the season.*

ABOVE, RIGHT *A willow ptarmigan* (Lagopus lagopus) *in white winter plumage.*

A shorttail weasel or ermine (Mustela erminea) *in summer fur. In winter, these quick, agile hunters change into white fur; only the tip of the tail is black. Lemmings and voles are their main prey.*

ABOVE *A snow goose* (Chen hyperborea) *and its young. This summer visitor builds its down-lined nest above the treeline.*

OPPOSITE *Two worried Kodiak bear* (Ursus arctos middendorffi) *cubs stand at a river's edge in Alaska while their mother fishes for salmon.*

ABOVE *In summer, the arctic fox* (Alopex lagopus) *hunts rodents and young birds.*

RIGHT *A brown lemming* (Lemmus trimucronatus) *leaves its tundra burrow to search for food. These small herbivores are the main prey of several arctic animals and birds, including the wolf and gyrfalcon.*

OPPOSITE *The red-throated loon* (Gavia stellata)*, a summer visitor to the Arctic, nests near ponds and small lakes.*

TOP *A furious parasitic jaeger* (Stercorarius parasiticus) *attacks an enemy approaching its tundra nest. Jaegers are skillful hunters, but they often prefer to rob gulls and terns of their prey.*

ABOVE *An arctic ground squirrel* (Citellus undulatus) *among fireweed* (Epilobium angustifolium). *In fall, these squirrels feed so energetically, they nearly double their weight. They hibernate for seven to eight months.*

LEFT *The Peary caribou* (Rangifer tarandus Pearyi) *is smaller and lighter in color than the barren-ground caribou. Its white coat of hollow hairs provides good protection from the winter temperatures on the high-arctic islands where it lives.*

ABOVE *Bull moose (Alces alces), weighing about 1,000 pounds, are formidable adversaries, often able to repel attacks by small wolf packs.*

OPPOSITE *A juvenile snowy owl (Nyctea scandiaca). These diurnal arctic owls feed mainly on lemmings and other rodents.*

154

A red fox (Vulpes fulva) *in winter. In recent decades, red foxes have moved farther and farther north into the realm of the much smaller arctic foxes.*

ABOVE *In the farthest north, on Ellesmere Island, a knot (*Calidris canutus*) settles upon its nest. In fall, the high-arctic knots migrate across Greenland to Iceland, rest and feed there for a while and then fly to Britain and Holland, where they spend the winter.*

LEFT *An arctic hare (*Lepus arcticus*) carefully grooms its large, furry hind paw. In the far north, these large hares remain white all year; in lower latitudes, their summer fur is brownish-gray.*

157

LEFT *A lone male musk-ox* (Ovibos moschatus) *on a hill above Mercy Bay on northern Banks Island in the Canadian Arctic. Most musk-oxen live in herds, but old bulls travel alone, at least during the fall rutting season.*

OVERLEAF *These young ruddy turnstones* (Arenaria interpres) *are well camouflaged in their arctic nest. Turnstones like rocky tidal shores, where they feed on small marine life.*

159

PART TWO

THE ARCTIC WILDERNESS

Massed common murres (Uria
aalge) *upon a remote brooding
island. The Labrador Current
carries icebergs past their island.*

CHAPTER 10

Wildlife of the Sea and Land

DR. THOR LARSEN

A VISITOR TO THE ARCTIC is often struck by the surprising abundance of plants, birds and mammals. But a closer look reveals that the number of non-migrating species is low. As a rule, the abundance of plant and animal species increases tenfold as we travel from the high Arctic toward temperate regions. The low number of arctic species is generally thought to be caused by rigorous living conditions. Poikilothermal animals — those with body temperatures and metabolisms that change as the environmental conditions change — cannot survive in the far north. Their blood and tissues freeze as the temperature drops below the freezing point. Consequently, typical poikilotherms such as lizards, snakes and frogs are lacking in these latitudes. On the other hand, homeothermal animals — those which maintain a relatively constant deep body temperature — can survive in the Arctic even when ambient temperatures change drastically.

Arctic birds and mammals are specialized for life in a harsh environment. Insulation against cold is a key factor in their survival. It has been shown that the skin temperature of large arctic mammals is usually only a few degrees lower than their deep body temperature, even when the air temperature is as low as $-40°F$. There can be a gradient of 125°F or more between skin and air temperatures. This demonstrates the excellent insulating efficiency of the fur of arctic animals. The musk-ox is a good example. It has a very dense layer of wool close to its body, which is covered and protected by an outer layer of very long hairs. The thick fur of the musk-ox makes it an impressive animal to meet on the tundra in midwinter. But if its fur were removed, the animal would be surprisingly small.

The coats of other arctic mammals are also designed for protection against cold. The caribou or reindeer's fur consists of

Two northern elephant seal (Mirounga angustirostris) *bulls fight for possession of a harem. Once nearly extinct, the population of these seals has increased sharply in recent years.*

long, hollow hairs, which trap the air and are therefore very good insulators. The polar bear's fur is even more ingenious. Its hairs are transparent. This allows light to penetrate through the fur down to the skin, which is black. In effect, the polar bear's pelt serves as a greenhouse. Heat and light penetrate the transparent hairs and are absorbed by the black skin surface. Very little heat escapes from the body again, because it is trapped by the dense fur. The result is that the polar bear can utilize and conserve maximum amounts of heat from the sun, thereby thriving even in extreme cold.

Bird feathers are also very efficient insulators against cold. The plumage of resident arctic birds tends to be more dense, and therefore more insulating, than the plumage of migratory birds. Birds can reduce heat loss when it becomes very cold by fluffing their feathers. When they also pull their legs up under their bodies and protect their heads by putting them under the feathers on their backs, they make the best possible use of their plumage.

In addition to fur and plumage, some arctic species have fat layers for protection against cold. The polar bear has a thick layer of blubber under its skin. Because it spends much of its life in the drift ice, the polar bear is forced to swim for long periods of time in ice-cold water. There, fur offers little or no protection. A human who falls into extremely cold water will freeze to death in a matter of minutes. But the polar bear can swim for hours among the ice floes, because its fat layer helps retain body heat. Some arctic ungulates — for example, the Svalbard reindeer — have a blubber layer which can be almost four inches thick. The blubber serves two functions in the reindeer. It protects against cold during long, harsh winters, and it provides a nutritional reserve. The reindeer uses a great deal of energy when it digs through the snow to find the remnants of last summer's vegetation. Sometimes it spends more energy digging than it obtains from eating what it finally finds. Under such conditions, the combined insulation and energy reserve in its blubber is needed in order for the animal to survive the winter. Most of the blubber is depleted by late spring, but intensive grazing on lush vegetation during the summer builds up a new deposit. Ptarmigans also have large fat deposits, which they can utilize in a similar way in the winter.

Arctic marine mammals live in a less extreme environment than land-living animals. Polar waters are normally close to, or slightly below, 32°F. The temperature gradients between the deep body temperatures of sea mammals and the temperature of the environment is therefore only half of what terrestrial animals sometimes experience. Seals, walruses and whales have

TOP *The arctic tern* (sterna paradi-saea) *breeds on coasts throughout the Arctic and sub-Arctic. In the fall, it migrates to the Antarctic.*

ABOVE *With a beakful of food for its ever-hungry young, a male snow bunting* (Plectrophenax nivalis) *pauses upon a rock near its nest.*

short hair or no hair at all on their skin. They are totally dependent upon a thick blubber layer for protection against cold. Since their skin is exposed, marine mammals must maintain a skin temperature that is high enough to prevent freezing and damage to tissues, but low enough to prevent excessive energy drain. Transport of heat from the warm body to the skin is regulated by a finely tuned blood circulation system. The result is a difference of almost 75°F between the deep body and skin temperatures.

Small arctic mammals such as lemmings and ground squirrels have neither blubber nor thick fur for insulation. Furthermore, their small size in itself creates additional heat conservation problems. A small body has a large surface in relation to its volume, therefore, more energy is needed to maintain a constant deep body temperature. Small mammals can partly solve their heat conservation problems by seeking shelter in burrows and nests. They can also use the excellent insulating properties of snow. The air temperature can be as low as −22°F, but it is normally only around the freezing point in the network of shallow tunnels dug by small rodents. They can live comfortably there, and feed and even breed in midwinter.

Some birds also utilize shelters, particularly at night. Tits and many other small birds spend the night in hollow trees, where they are protected against wind and where their own body heat increases the environmental temperature. Snow buntings, ptarmigans and grouse dig holes in the snow, often so deep that their bodies are entirely covered. Scandinavian farmers and trappers have known about this behavior for centuries. When they ski through the winter forests in the early morning, they can locate ptarmigans and grouse by looking for small mounds in the snow.

Polar bear females use the insulating properties of the snow when they give birth. In late fall, they dig maternity dens in snowbanks. There, the cubs are born in midwinter, almost hairless and without any protective subcutaneous fat. However, the temperature in the den is normally not below the freezing point, even when it is −20°F or colder outside. In addition, the mother can offer a favorable microclimate for her cubs as they huddle against her belly between her large legs. Finally, the polar bear's milk has a high fat content and is very rich in nutrients, thus the cubs can afford to use more energy to sustain body temperatures when ambient temperatures are low. When the bear cubs emerge from the dens in mid-March, they have developed a thick fur.

The polar bear's problem is often not conserving heat, but getting rid of it. They are frequently seen resting in pits or shallow

A fulmar (Fulmarus glacialis) paddles across the smooth sea off northern Greenland. Fulmars have the longest breeding season of all northern birds; parents arrive at breeding ledges in early May, and some chicks fledge as late as the end of September.

dens in snowbanks when they are on land in the summer. When summer temperatures rise, the snow offers a highly needed cooling place. If the snow has melted, bears are often seen sprawled on their backs, with their legs wide apart to expose their bellies, which have relatively little hair. The polar bear generally moves slowly and spends a lot of time resting. When it hunts for seals, its chase is fast, but short. Unlike wolves and some large cats, the polar bear cannot run for long periods of time, because it can become overheated. If a bear is chased by an aircraft or a snowmobile, it will soon dive into open water to cool off. If there is no water available, it may stop and simply sit down. Some observers have misinterpreted this behavior, saying it is caused by the bear's natural calm and lack of fear. In reality, a polar bear that is chased in this way is probably afraid, overheated and exhausted. Observers and eager photographers should remember this and avoid chasing bears and other large arctic mammals. A prolonged chase may exhaust an animal with a dense fur coat, or possibly cause its death.

Arctic animals sometimes change their posture with increasing cold or wind. Polar bears turn on their bellies for better protection, and when the weather is inclement, they curl up. Arctic dogs pull their feet up against their bellies and cover their noses with their tails. A thermometer inserted in the center of a dog in this posture may register a temperature only a few degrees lower than the dog's body temperature, while the air temperature may be $-4°F$ or lower. Snow does not melt on their bodies because of the insulating properties of their fur. Such curled-up dogs can sometimes be completely covered by falling or drifting snow, which offers additional protection. Arctic foxes and wolves behave in a similar way.

Energy drain is so high in winter that nearly all arctic warm-blooded animals must lower their general activity level when it is cold. Low ambient temperatures require an increased metabolism in order to maintain a constant deep body temperature. Consequently, the animals must burn more fat, which is stored in their bodies, or eat more. For this reason, arctic animals avoid unnecessary activity during the winter. Almost all their time is spent resting or feeding. Disturbances of arctic wildlife in winter can be fatal. To avoid intruders, they must spend a lot of energy flying or running. The result can be a severe reduction of their fat reserves and an inability to compensate for the energy losses through feeding. Arctic birds and mammals commonly lose weight in the winter, because energy requirements are too high to be maintained by normal feeding. Small arctic rodents can lose as much as 40 percent of their maximum summer weights. Some species even have to use energy reserves

A parasitic jaeger swoops down to pick a morsel from the sea's surface.

in summer. When the female eider duck is brooding, she must maintain a normal deep body temperature in order to avoid cooling her eggs. She therefore spends all her time on the nest. As she does not feed in this period, she loses up to 45 percent of her body weight. When the eggs are hatched, she is in a critical state and must leave for the sea with her clutch to feed. If eiders are disturbed in their colonies during this period, they may be forced to use so much additional energy that they will die before the eggs are hatched or shortly afterward.

Many arctic birds face serious problems in their efforts to maintain body heat, particularly the small bird species. Small birds have a higher metabolic rate than large birds. They need food more often to support their energy requirements and to stay alive. Energy drain can be so high in extreme cold that some small birds would die if they could not compensate for it. One survival method is increasing metabolism and thereby heat production in order to compensate for heat loss. Shivering is one way to do it. More muscle activity is used, which yields more body heat, but that leads to a higher energy consumption, which again requires more food. This can be a problem, particularly in winter when food is scarce and when feeding is limited to only a few hours of daylight. Another method is to lower the metabolic rate by lowering the body temperature. Some small birds are able to enter a state at night that is comparable to hibernation. The result is energy savings that can be as high as 15 to 30 percent. When small arctic birds combine several energy-saving methods, such as fluffing of feathers, seeking shelter and lowering of metabolic rate, they can save as much as 50 percent of their normal energy consumption.

If you take off your gloves on a cold arctic day, you will notice that the falling snow melts on your hands. Soon your fingers hurt and become numb. After a while, the cold may cause frostbite, and if exposure lasts, skin and tissue can be seriously damaged. We cannot live and work in the Arctic without effective protection. How is it then possible for arctic sledge dogs to walk in very cold snow seemingly without being bothered by it? How can ducks, geese and gulls stand on an ice floe for hours, evidently without any problems? The dog's feet do not melt the snow, nor do the bird's feet freeze to the ice or melt it.

If we measure the skin temperatures along the legs of arctic birds and mammals, we discover that there is a temperature gradient along the leg, from the body toward the ground. Under the soles and paws of such animals, the skin temperature is normally only slightly above freezing. This means that the feet of arctic animals maintain a temperature high enough to prevent freezing and damage of tissue, but low enough to prevent

Whistling swan (Olor columbianus)
cygnets upon a tundra meadow.

melting of snow and ice and thereby heat loss. Arctic birds and mammals have what is called a counter-current system in their legs. Blood pumped from the heart has a normal deep body temperature. However, the arteries carrying the outflowing blood are surrounded by veins carrying blood back from the feet and the distant parts of the limbs. As blood flows toward the feet, it gives off heat to blood which flows back to the

168

body. Consequently, the outflowing blood is gradually cooled by emitting heat until it reaches the feet. There, it has given off so much heat that it has a temperature only slightly above freezing. But on its way back, it is gradually warmed by warm blood pouring out to the limbs. And when it returns to the body cavity, it has a temperature that differs little from what it was when it left the heart earlier. This causes a gradual cooling of legs and feet, which is necessary in order to avoid tissue damage. The system ensures that very little body energy is lost to the environment.

Counter-current systems are also present in the noses of some arctic mammals. When you walk on the tundra on a very cold day, small clouds of water vapor form each time you exhale. Much heat and water is lost through your breathing; hence you need to eat and drink more when it is cold. But under the same conditions, a reindeer exhales very little vapor. Cold air inhaled by the reindeer passes thin veins in the nose and is warmed before it reaches the lungs. Warm air which is exhaled gives off heat gradually as it passes the same veins before it leaves the body. The result is the same as in the legs of arctic mammals and birds. The heat and water is conserved within the body, and only a minimum is lost to the environment.

When seals and whales are resting on the ice, the skin on their bellies is in contact with the ice, while the rest of their bodies may be exposed to the heat from the sun. Such marine mammals are able to alter their circulatory efficiency and therefore the thermoregulation of different parts of their bodies under such conditions. Such differences may change as the animals change their position on the ice or slip into the water. The thermal conditions in seal and whale flippers can change faster and more extremely than in the rest of the body. It has been shown that there are counter-current systems in the extremities of seals and whales comparable to those of land-living mammals and birds. Flippers can serve as effective heat dissipators when environmental conditions make it necessary.

It has been claimed that ecosystems in the Arctic are more fragile than they are in other latitudes with more favorable living conditions. This is only partly true. Birds and mammals of the Arctic are true opportunists. Not only are they well adapted to a difficult life under marginal conditions, but they are also able to cope with environmental conditions that change suddenly and drastically. Arctic ecosystems may be more able to meet changing living conditions than previously thought, but they also have their limits, which must be recognized. Our new knowledge must be used wisely if we are to manage the Arctic and its exciting life forms properly.

The snow-streaked mountains of
Attu in the Aleutians soar above
valleys and slopes carpeted with
flowers.

CHAPTER 11

Plants of the Arctic and Sub-Arctic

DR. FRANS WIELGOLASKI

MANY PEOPLE expect the Arctic to be a region of snow and ice with no plants at all. This is true for more than half the year, and in some cases for all of it, but many areas of the Arctic and sub-Arctic support a variety of plants, which have adapted to the short growing season and low average temperatures of the far north.

Even trees are found in the subarctic region. In the coastal areas of northern Scandinavia, Iceland and parts of eastern Siberia along the Bering Sea, broad-leaved deciduous birch tree species form the northern treeline. Along the edge of the northern treeline of Canada and Alaska, as well as in most parts of eastern Siberia, scattered coniferous trees are found in what is called the forest tundra. In North America, spruce trees are common in the sub-Arctic; in Siberia, various deciduous larch species form the treeline.

The northernmost trees in the world are members of the larch genus. Although they are called trees, they are frequently less than three feet in height. Their stems are crooked, and their branches lie close to the ground. Almost hidden in a moss carpet, they are surrounded by plants that prefer a thin snow layer, which disappears relatively early in the spring.

A thin snow cover and low winter temperatures generally indicate that there is permafrost in the ground. Only the upper soil layer melts in the summer. This often thin layer of approximately 20 inches or less is enough for some tree species, such as the larch and spruce, to establish themselves. It is incredible that plants can survive with their roots growing down into cold and often frozen soil. However, even in summer, these plants may have problems. Due to the permafrost layer below the surface of the soil, the vertical drainage of water is so slow that the plants are nearly drowned because there is little oxygen reaching their roots. This often results in slow growth.

The winter temperatures along the subarctic coasts are generally not so low as in subarctic inland areas. This is particularly true along the North Atlantic coasts, due to the Gulf Stream. In January, the average temperature does not fall below 32°F at 68°N on the outer Lofoten Islands off Norway. Consequently, no permafrost is found on these islands. Although the growth period is fairly long, the summer temperatures are never high. The humidity and wind speed, on the other hand, are usually high year-round. Coniferous trees, particularly the evergreen ones, are injured by strong winds and salt spray. However, the leaf bud break of birch trees in spring seems to be favored by high humidity; this may account for the good growth of these species in subarctic marine climates.

The forest tundra of the subarctic region is usually a mosaic of scattered trees or clumps of trees rising above other vegetation. To the south, it gradually changes into closed forest, the taiga, as the climate gets less severe. The northern parts of these forests are sometimes called low subarctic regions. Due to greater continentality and deeper soils across the Soviet Union, it has been easier to define zones of subarctic and arctic vegetation there than in other northern countries. In Canada, for example, the last glaciation removed much of the soil. Differences in soil, climate and topography across arctic Canada have caused a mosaic pattern of vegetation instead of clearly defined zones.

The forest tundra may resemble savanna vegetation. There is usually a well-developed vegetation cover below the trees. In habitats with adequate supplies of water for plant growth throughout the growing season, there are several shrubs, sometimes three to nine feet high, of various species of polar birch. Several species of willow also grow in the zone, particularly where the soil is deep and rich in nutrients. They are therefore most abundant on moist slopes and in valleys. The tallest shrubs are found in the bottoms of sheltered valleys. Tall herbaceous broad-leaved plants and grasses grow below this shrub layer, and often a thick moss cover is found on the bottom. This type of subarctic plant community is fascinating. It is unexpectedly dense and very difficult to walk through.

Although the forest tundra of the sub-Arctic covers large areas in some parts of the world, most people think of the treeless tundra when they think of the Arctic. Scientists have studied the reasons for the position of the treeline in relation to prevailing climates. Generally, temperature during the growing season seems to be the most important single factor for the distribution of woody plants. For example, vegetative growth of the Norway

A slowly disintegrating whale bone on northern Baffin Island provides nutrients to a small cluster of plants.

spruce and Scotch pine stops if the average temperature of the four summer months (June to September) is below 47°F. For seeds to ripen, even higher temperatures are necessary. Willows grow at temperatures above 42°F in the same four summer months.

For that reason, willows often grow far north of the treeline, but their height decreases to the north. Just before they disappear, they are less than ten inches high, whereas the same species close to the treeline might be three to ten feet high. The willow thicket belt is often called low arctic tundra, and the areas where only dwarf shrubs are found is called high arctic tundra. It is not only the shrubs that diminish to the north, but also all herbaceous broad-leaved plants and grasses that need the shelter from the shrubs. Two vegetation types predominate in the high Arctic: wet sedge-moss communities and dwarf shrub heaths in less extreme climates and in relatively dry, poor soil. Both are also common in the low Arctic.

At the highest latitudes, the vegetation cover is scarce or missing entirely. Dr. Vera Alexandrova of the Soviet Union found that cryptogams — particularly lichens, but also mosses — dominate these northernmost ice-free areas, which are often called polar deserts. Between the polar desert and the high Arctic, some scientists define a transition zone called polar semi-desert. The percentage of mosses may be as high as in the true polar desert, but the amount of lichens is lower and the amount of flowering plants is higher.

Of the flowering plants, species with appressed leaf rosettes and cushion and other mat-forming plants tend to occupy the

173

zones of lowest temperatures. Usually they are found in moderately rich and moist soil along drainage channels. Some grasses and sedges survive very well in extremely low summer temperatures. However, shrubs, even dwarf species, are generally absent from the regions with the lowest summer temperatures. They are not able to survive in polar deserts and semi-deserts, nor in the coldest parts of the high Arctic. Evergreen shrubs tend to dominate the most nutrient-poor communities of the low Arctic; on very dry and windswept ridges, evergreen dwarf shrubs are found.

It is obvious that some plant groups and some species within each group are better adapted to extreme environments than others. The ability to maintain growth in low temperatures is one of the most important adaptations for plants in the Arctic. Many flowering plants as well as mosses and lichen species in the tundra have positive net photosynthesis (the net accumulation of dry matter) even far below the freezing point. Scientists have discovered that the lichen *Cetraria nivalis*, which is common on nearly snow-free, windswept ridges both in alpine and arctic regions, continues growth down to −4°F in subarctic Finland! Although this indicates that lichens may continue net photosynthesis at lower temperatures than any other plants, some mosses have also been found to have similar abilities. They have continued to grow at almost 14°F. At these low temperatures, the growth is very small, but at 32°F the photosynthetic rates are substantial in both lichens and mosses. In some lichen species — for instance, in a Svalbard strain of *Stereocaulon paschale* — the optimum temperature for growth is close to 32°F, an amazing adaptation to arctic conditions.

The above-ground parts of several of the beautiful flowering plants of the Arctic (the mountain sorrel, trailing azalea and glacier buttercup, for example) also continue to grow at temperatures down to nearly 23°F. Even the roots of these plants grow at lower temperatures than in temperate regions, often close to 32°F. Their optimum temperatures for growth, however, are surprisingly high, above the air temperatures they are normally exposed to in the Arctic.

The glacier buttercup accumulates nutrients and carbohydrates produced by the photosynthesis of several years in its vegetative parts before flowers are produced. A similar accumulation is found in other perennial tundra plants; for example, in the herblike dwarf willow. This is an adaptation for the extremely short growing season often found in the Arctic. Because it may also take more than one year from the initiation of flowers to ripe seeds, the life cycles of plants in the Arctic may be much longer than the life cycles of similar species at lower latitudes.

Arctic vegetation is often extremely sensitive to small differences in temperature. The leaf structure of plants can influence light interception, heat interception from the ground and heat loss from the plant. The greatest solar interception, and thus highest leaf temperature, is generally found when radiation reaches the leaves at right angles. At high latitudes, the solar angle is low and temperatures are frequently below optimum for plant growth, at least in moist situations. This means that the presence of vertical leaves in arctic regions may be linked to increased production.

Many plants in the Arctic have nearly vertical leaves, especially grasses and sedges. It is not surprising that high photosynthesis is found at high latitudes in single-shooted species within these groups. Here the shading effect is moderate even for the inner leaves. As these plants usually grow in very wet conditions, the leaf temperature is seldom too high, even on the nearly vertical unshaded leaves, because of cooling by transpiration.

Plants with leaves near the soil surface always receive a heat surplus from the ground during the day, particularly if the soil is dry. For this reason, these species normally have high temperature optima for photosynthesis. However, some (the mountain avens, for example) must close the stomata on their leaves in order to prevent the loss of too much water by transpiration in high temperatures. Others (many dwarf shrubs, tufted grasses and crowberries, for example) prevent too much water loss by the accumulation of several dead leaves among the living ones. Because of the slow rate of decomposition in the Arctic's low temperatures, dead leaves will remain on these plants for several years. Arctic plants also lessen water loss by reducing leaf size or by producing a dense hair layer, which helps to store incoming heat as well.

Arctic plants with nearly horizontal leaves use another strategy for protection. The mountain sorrel and the glacier buttercup are examples of plants with nearly horizontal leaves, particularly in spring. They normally grow in moist soil and have an important growth period in early spring just after the snow melts. During these moist periods, an increased temperature may be favorable, and this may be obtained from the transmittal of heat from the soil to the horizontal leaves.

Rapid growth in spring as soon as the snow melts and during long periods of daylight is the way many arctic plants have adapted to the short growing season. This is very important in snow beds, where the combination of extremely late snow melt and frozen soil results in very little photosynthesis before all the snow is melted. In some cases, however, growth starts even before the snow has melted due to the penetration of sunlight through the snow cover. Plant growth under the snow takes place only if the upper soil layer is not frozen; this is often the case in late winter. The growth explosion in spring is mainly an elongation of small leaves formed the previous fall and protected through the winter by bud scales and sheaths at the bases of the shoots. This elongation depends upon a rapid and abundant supply of both energy and nutrients from a well-developed winter storage system.

The flowers of the glacier buttercup, mountain avens and several other arctic plants have a parabolic form. This is used to collect as much sunlight as possible. Some of these flowers also change their direction with the time of day so that they are always open toward the sun. This may be particularly important for white flowers, which reflect more radiation than dark-colored flowers. But why then are there white flowers in the Arctic? One reason may be their attractiveness to insects necessary for their pollination.

In extreme climatic conditions, sufficient energy may not be available to store nutrients or to transport carbohydrates and minerals to and from the leaves in spring and fall. Plants in the high arctic polar desert, for example, are often adapted to reduce translocation by keeping their green leaves year-round. This is the case for many of the polar desert herbaceous broad-leaved plants, grasses and sedges, which do not have the high root mass compared to tops observed in the less extreme arctic regions. Instead, the energy and nutrients are stored in the green leaves throughout the winter. In the Canadian high arctic tundra, the lower parts of the leaves in the middle of densely tufted Hepburn's sedge or nard live four to six years. In some plants in the high Arctic and polar deserts, many leaves are reddish in winter but do not die. They quickly turn green again in spring. In the same species at lower latitudes, the leaves normally die during the winter.

Evergreen dwarf shrubs are common in dry, nutrient-poor and windswept ridges in the low Arctic. Their leaves remain active for two to three years. Because the leaves stay more or less green in winter, the bud break of evergreens is later than that of deciduous plants. Evergreens can utilize the radiation for photosynthesis in the old leaves. Nutrients also may be moved from the old leaves to the new growth places when needed. This internal nutrient circulation system is an adaptation in evergreen plants for growth on nutrient-poor soil.

The environmental factors in the Arctic thus select for various plant types through adaptation and specialization to the conditions found there.

A BRIEF FLOWERING

ABOVE *Cottongrass (*Eriphorum sp.) *is a northern sedge. The "cotton" is not the plant's flower but a covering for its fruit. The minute green flowers are barely visible.*

LEFT *Ruby-tipped arctic marsh willow (*Salix arctophila) *catkins glow in the slanting rays of the midnight sun.*

OPPOSITE *Arctic poppies (*Papaver radicatum) *in the midnight sun. The fine hairs on the stems help to capture the sun's warmth.*

OVERLEAF *A bog dotted with black spruce (*Picea mariana) *in early September.*

TOP *Less than 600 miles from the North Pole, a deceptively delicate-looking butterfly sips at a mountain avens* (Dryas integrifolia) *bloom.*

ABOVE *A tiny wedge-leaved primrose* (Primula cuneifolia).

LEFT *An Alaskan landscape filled with poppies.*

ABOVE *A cluster of alpine forget-me-nots* (Eritrichium *sp.*).

OPPOSITE, ABOVE *The spider saxifrage* (Saxifraga flagellaris) *multiplies vegetatively. Scarlet runners move outward from the parent plant. Wherever they touch suitable soil, they take root and grow new plants.*

OPPOSITE, BELOW *Lousewort* (Pedicularis capitata).

ABOVE *Orange groundsel* (Senecio fuscatus) *and monkshood* (Aconitum delphinifolium) *on Herschel Island in the Beaufort Sea. Over 200 species of vascular plants grow on this island.*

OPPOSITE *Hairy lupine* (Lupinus sericeus) *leaves and stems covered with myriad water droplets.*

ABOVE *Cloudberry* (Rubus chamaemorus), *a member of the raspberry family, grows on mountains, along rocky shores and in bogs.*

LEFT *Birches, larches and pines dominate Siberia's taiga, which covers more than 1,900 million acres. It is the largest forest region on earth.*

189

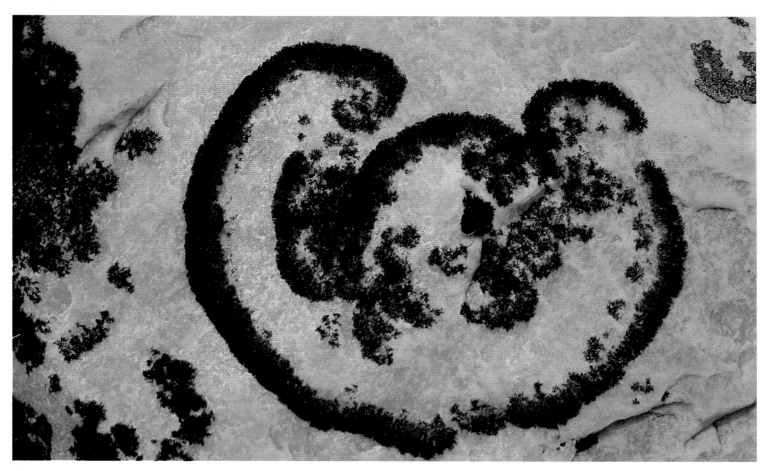

ABOVE *Like graceful black writing upon white quartzite, crustose lichen covers a rock. Lichens are immensely hardy, but most grow very slowly, some at the rate of 1 centimeter in 1,000 years.*

LEFT *A bumblebee gathers nectar from an arctic dandelion (*Teraxacum *sp.). Since bulk conserves warmth, the bumblebees of the farthest north are big and very furry.*

OPPOSITE *Purple saxifrage (*Saxifraga oppositifolia)*, among the hardiest and most common of arctic flowers, bloom in a rock niche.*

OVERLEAF *High on a pressure ridge, an Inuk hunter scans the ice with his telescope in search of polar bears. Although the telescope's range is greater, most Inuit now prefer to use binoculars.*

191

PART THREE

PEOPLE OF THE FAR NORTH

ABOVE *A Polar Inuit child in northwest Greenland plays on the ice. The handle of the dog team whip serves to bat snowballs.*

LEFT *A Polar Inuit youngster in northwest Greenland brings gloves and binoculars to her father, who is about to leave on an early summer trip.*

OPPOSITE *A Canadian Inuk chats with visitors.*

ABOVE *A Siberian science class.*

RIGHT *A boy from Baffin Island is warmly dressed in fur-rimmed parka.*

OPPOSITE *The experiences of a long and often hard life are etched in the serene face of an Inuit woman from Canada's central Arctic.*

197

LEFT *A Skoltt Lapp woman in traditional headdress at a funeral. Once a coastal people, these Lapps were resettled in Finland after World War II.*

BELOW *In Norwegian Lapland, a mother feeds her child.*

OPPOSITE *A Canadian Inuit artist displays her work.*

A stone ambush used by caribou hunters long ago upon the rocky tundra of Canada's Barren Grounds.

CHAPTER 12

The Ancient Arctic

DR. ROBERT McGHEE

HUMANS ARE TROPICAL ANIMALS. Our ancient ape-like ancestors first stood upright, developed large brains and learned how to use sticks and stones as tools, in the forests and savannas of the equatorial belt. It is not surprising that the tundras, polar deserts and ice fields of the Arctic were the last major regions of the world to be occupied by humans. Yet the Arctic has been important to the development of human life on earth. Through the arctic environment of ancient Beringia, people first moved from the Old World to the New. In the arctic regions surrounding Baffin Bay and the Labrador Sea, the westward expansion of the medieval Norse first encountered the eastward expansion of aboriginal North Americans, completing the chain of human movement around the globe. Perhaps most important, the periodic expansion of arctic environments into more southerly latitudes must have forced early humans to develop more sophisticated methods of survival and accelerated the development of technology and technique.

The development of human beings and human cultures occurred over the past two or three million years, a time known as the Pleistocene, the period of ice ages. During the brief interglacial periods between ice ages, ancestral humans who had learned to survive the cold, glacial conditions of mid-latitude Europe and Asia must have been tempted northward, following the herds of animals which fed on lands recently freed from beneath the continental glaciers. For people who could hunt large animals, and who had clothing, tents and fire to protect them from the wind and cold, the Arctic was an excellent place to live. Many northern animals are found in dense seasonal aggregations, which can be very efficiently exploited by hunters. Contrary to the ideas proposed by some early historians and anthropologists, the aboriginal peoples of the far north were not exiled to marginal regions by more powerful southern neighbors; since at least the last ice age, hunters have been attracted to northern regions by the animal resources of the Arctic.

Our earliest archaeological picture of northern peoples, living ways of life as sophisticated as those of recent northern hunters, is during the last ice age in Europe, between approximately 25,000 and 12,000 years ago. The Upper Paleolithic peoples hunted across the tundra and taiga landscapes of central and western Europe, preying on herd animals as large as the mammoth, and leaving behind them the painted caves which, since their discovery during the last century, have testified to the spiritual richness of our remote ancestors' lives.

Across central and eastern Asia, similar Upper Paleolithic groups hunted northward into the forests and steppe-tundras of Siberia. Our archaeological knowledge of these regions is much poorer than that of Europe, but cave sites and river terraces along the Aldan River show that people using chipped stone tools and hunting reindeer, bison, horse and mammoth were living as far north as present-day Yakutsk, close to the Arctic Circle, by the beginning of the last ice age about 35,000 years ago. At some time during the glaciation, related groups spread eastward to Kamchatka, and northward to the Indigirka River, where a site occupied by mammoth hunters was found only 90 miles from the Arctic coast.

Farther to the east, related groups discovered a new land, which grew as the glaciers advanced, lowering the level of the sea to expose the beds of continental shelves. This was Beringia, a level plain linking the Chukchi Peninsula of Siberia to Alaska, and extending eastward through unglaciated valleys as far as northwestern Canada. The cold and dry Beringian plain was home to most of the animals that now occupy arctic regions, as well as species that were to become extinct at the end of the ice age.

We know little of these earliest occupants of far northwestern North America. In physical appearance, they likely resembled their descendants, the New World Indians. They were big-game hunters, whose weapons and knives were tipped or edged with sharp blades of chipped stone. They must have worn animal skins and may have sheltered in conical tents covered with skins. They probably brought to North America the basic beliefs once shared by northern peoples of both the Old and New Worlds: a shamanistic religion and world view; magic practices to cure illness, control the weather and secure game; and an intense respect for the bear, manifested in ceremonial treatment of bears killed in the hunt.

Archaeological evidence for the presence of such people is found in the Bluefish Caves of the northern Yukon. In this small group of limestone rock shelters are stone tools (similar to those used in Siberia at the time) associated with the bones of now extinct animals of between 15,000 and 20,000 years ago. At some time after 15,000 years ago, the continental glaciers began to retreat, and a corridor opened between the ice sheets of the Canadian Shield and those of the Rocky Mountains. Some of the inhabitants of Beringia moved south and began to hunt along the southern edge of the glaciers, in what is today southern Canada and the northern United States.

The continental glaciers melted rapidly during the first few millenniums of the present interglacial. By about 8,000 years ago, they had retreated to approximately their present positions on mountains and high-arctic islands. The arctic tundras and subarctic forests also moved northward, as did the animals of the tundras, forests and northern seas. In both Eurasia and North America, hunters followed these animals into the higher latitudes, establishing occupation across the forests of Scandinavia, Siberia and northern North America. Here they developed the ways of life characteristic of northern forest peoples up to the present century — living in skin tents and winter lodges built of logs, fishing with hooks and gill nets, hunting the caribou (reindeer) and the moose (elk), traveling summer rivers by canoe and the snows of winter by ski and sled in the Old World or by snowshoe and toboggan in the New. Although some of these groups spent summers in the tundra, usually following the migratory caribou north of the treeline, most appear to have retreated from the first storms of winter to the forests, which provided necessary shelter and fuel.

By 8,000 years ago, the arctic regions fringing the northern coasts of both Eurasia and North America, as well as the islands to the north, were very much as they are today. On the relatively warm and ice-free coasts of Labrador and Norway, hunting peoples moved northward into the tundra zones, apparently depending heavily on the resources of the sea to survive north of the treeline. Yet for the next 4,000 years, most of the Arctic remained empty of human habitation. Not until approximately 4,000 years ago did a group of humans learn to build a way of life that allowed them to remain in the Arctic throughout the year.

It is an accident of archaeology that the best evidence relating to these people comes from arctic Canada and Greenland, where they are known to archaeologists as Paleoeskimos. In fact, the adaptations that allowed them to move into arctic regions were almost certainly developed in northern Siberia, although few archaeological sites relating to these people are known from the area. Similarly, Alaska has produced little evidence of early Paleoeskimo occupation, although it must have been on the route the Paleoeskimos followed from Siberia to arctic Canada.

The early Paleoeskimos of arctic Canada and Greenland left behind them archaeological sites which testify to their unique way of life, so different from that of the Indian inhabitants of the northern forests. The remains of their camps appear today as scattered boulders and stone slabs on the barren beaches of arctic coasts, littered with the bleached bones of the animals they killed and the stone tools they used to tip weapons and cutting tools. They were masters of the difficult art of chipping flintlike stone to produce tiny, almost jewel-like points for arrows and harpoons, scrapers for working skins, carving tools for making artifacts of bone or antler, and razor-blade-like slivers of stone known as microblades, made by a specialized Asiatic technique and mounted in handles to be used as knives. Their stone tools are so unique that these people have been given an archaeological name, the Arctic Small Tool Tradition, and it is the similarity of form between these tools and those used in northern Siberia at the time that suggests a Siberian origin for the Paleoeskimos. Their dwellings, as reconstructed from the rocks used to hold the edges of tents and form the interior arrangements, are also reminiscent of Asiatic forms. The standard Paleoeskimo dwelling seems to have been a skin-covered tent, with a central box-hearth built of stone slabs. From either side of the hearth, a line of upright slabs extended to the front and rear of the tent, forming a mid-passage, which may have served as a work or storage area separated from the sleeping areas on either side. The traditional tent used by the Lapps (Saami) of northern Scandinavia had an identical interior arrangement.

The lives of the early Paleoeskimos must have been considerably less comfortable and secure than those of later occupants of arctic North America. They seem to have lived throughout the year in skin tents, with heat and light provided only by an occasional small fire of driftwood, the tiny stems of arctic willow, and the bones and fat of the animals they hunted. Although they were equipped with bows and arrows — and were indeed the first North American people to use such weapons — their other means of hunting were much less sophisticated than those of later groups. They apparently had no boats, nor did they use the float-harpoon equipment which allowed the recent Inuit to effectively hunt sea mammals larger than those that could be easily held and retrieved by hand. In most areas they showed a preference for hunting caribou, musk-

Petroglyph masks incised into a soapstone outcrop on Qikertaaluk Island, Hudson Strait, off arctic Quebec. Believed to be of Dorset culture origin, these masks are probably about 1,000 years old and are the only Inuit petroglyphs ever found.

oxen and small game, supplemented by fishing and some coastal sealing. However, some groups did survive in areas where their economy was based largely on the hunting of sea mammals, which must have been done with hand-held harpoons and spears from the shore or from the sea ice. Although the archaeological remains of their camps are very meager, suggesting short-term occupations by tiny groups of people, they spread over vast regions in Greenland and Canada.

In the centuries after 500 B.C., the technology of the Paleoeskimos underwent a marked change. The most basic change was an increased emphasis on the hunting of sea mammals. Oil lamps carved from soapstone, and used for burning sea mammal oil to provide heat and light, appeared for the first time. This allowed the occupation of tightly closed and insulated winter dwellings, such as the snow house, which may have been invented at this time. In some areas, large semi-subterranean houses with walls of rock and turf were used. Settlements became larger and more permanent, apparently as a result of increased hunting efficiency. The degree of change is such that archaeologists gave a new name to these later Paleoeskimos: the Dorset culture.

The Dorset culture developed in the eastern Arctic during a period when the climate was rapidly becoming colder. For an ice-hunting people, such a change may have provided greater hunting opportunities, a challenge to the usual assumption that warmer climates make living conditions easier for northern peoples. The Dorset people spread south to Newfoundland and north to Ellesmere Island and northern Greenland.

The Paleoeskimos were the rulers of arctic North America for a period of more than 3,000 years. Over this time, in almost complete isolation from other human societies, they developed a unique adaptation to the arctic environment, involving not only technology but also a belief system which enabled human survival in a world lacking most of the elements necessary to human culture in more favored regions. Similar peoples must have been doing similar things in the Old World, although we lack the archaeological knowledge to reconstruct their ways of life. We do know that by about 4,000 years ago, people with a culture related to that of the early Paleoeskimos had occupied the arctic coast of Siberia and crossed the sea ice to occupy Wrangel Island, an island over 60 miles north of the Siberian mainland. In Svalbard (Spitsbergen), possible stone tools have been collected from elevated beaches, which would have formed the shore around 4,000 years ago, hinting at the possibility that hunters may also have reached this isolated archipelago.

While the Paleoeskimos and related peoples held the farthest

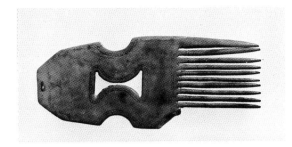

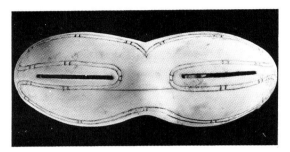

TOP *A woman's ivory comb, Thule culture, Bathurst Island, Canada.*

MIDDLE *An ivory winged object of unknown function, Old Bering Sea culture, Little Diomede Island, Alaska.*

BOTTOM *Ivory snow goggles, Thule culture, Devon Island, Canada.*

fringes of the Arctic, other groups were developing more sophisticated ways of life in a few rich areas along the southern margins of the arctic zone. In the Old World, our best evidence of such a development is from the northern coast of Norway. Here, hunters of the Komsa culture, who had inhabited the area since shortly after the end of the ice age, were gradually developing technology and techniques that allowed a marked population increase and a more sedentary and secure lifestyle. By about 5,000 years ago, they were living in large villages of permanent houses built from stone, turf and logs, each capable of sheltering two or more families. The bones of seals, dolphins and whales are prominent in the refuse middens of these houses, whose occupants had almost certainly learned the techniques of driving herds of small whales into shallow waters where they could be slaughtered. In order to do so, they must have had efficient boats, probably small plank-built craft similar to those used by the Neolithic and Bronze Age farming peoples of southern Scandinavia. Contact with the south is also evidenced by the introduction of pottery by at least 5,000 years ago, and later the appearance of imported items of metal.

It has been suggested that another and more important idea may have been imported from the agricultural areas of Europe: that of herding, rather than hunting, reindeer. In historic times, the herding of domestic reindeer was the economic base for most peoples of northern Europe and Siberia, providing greater economic security than that available to the hunting peoples of northern North America. Despite the importance of this invention, it is difficult to determine archaeologically where and when the practice began: reindeer bones are common in the old settlements of the north, but it is impossible to distinguish between the bones of a wild reindeer killed with an arrow and those of a domestic animal killed with a knife.

The coast of the Bering Sea, half a world away from northern Scandinavia, is the other region of the Arctic where archaeological evidence of important developments in the prehistoric past has been found. Since at least 3,000 years ago, the peoples living around this shallow and sea-mammal-rich body of water absorbed technologies and ideas emanating from the Bronze- and Iron-Age cultures of Siberia, as well as those moving up the Pacific coasts from the ancient civilizations of China and Japan and from the Indians of the northwest coast of North America. By at least 2,000 years ago, skin-covered boats had been developed, including the single-man hunting kayak and the large umiak. Large permanent villages composed of turf-covered log houses were established. Here the people passed the winters in ceremonial activities, feasting on the meat of seals and whales

A 17th-century drawing of two Lapps and a pack reindeer.

killed in the summer hunt, their houses warmed and lighted by the oil of sea mammals burning in pottery lamps. The celebrated art of the Old Bering Sea culture was developed, involving fine sculptures in ivory and elaborately decorated hunting weapons, carved with tools of iron obtained from the metal-using peoples of Siberia. By 1,500 years ago, the Asiatic recurved bow, armor constructed from slats of bone, and probably the techniques of Asiatic warfare had been adopted. With a secure economy based on the hunting of sea mammals, and with the equipment and knowledge necessary to wage successful warfare, the ancestral Eskimos of the Bering Sea area were in a position to expand their territory.

The occasion for such expansion seems to have come about 1,000 years ago, when the Medieval Warm Period was producing milder temperatures and less sea ice across the arctic world. For a people whose way of life was adapted to the open-water hunting of sea mammals, these conditions provided an opportunity to expand greatly their range of occupation. On the northern coast of Siberia, Eskimos pressed westward to at least the mouth of the Kolyma River. On the Pacific coast of North America, they displaced the previous occupants of Kodiak Island and the adjacent south coast of Alaska. Their greatest expansion, however, was eastward across the Arctic coasts of North America to Greenland. The eastward movement seems to have occurred very rapidly, following a route along the coasts of the Beaufort Sea, Amundsen Gulf and Parry Channel to the Thule district of northwestern Greenland, where the discovery of their archaeological remains led to the migrants being named the Thule culture Inuit. By about 1200, the Thule people had spread over most of arctic Canada and Greenland; southwestern Greenland was in the hands of recent Norse immigrants from Iceland, and Labrador remained the last outpost of Dorset Paleoeskimo occupation until about 1500.

Elsewhere in arctic Canada, the Paleoeskimo way of life disappeared, as the Dorset people were either killed, driven into areas where they could not survive or perhaps occasionally absorbed into the society of the Inuit invaders. The Thule people brought with them from Alaska the technology that allowed a much richer way of life than that of the Paleoeskimos. They successfully hunted animals as large as the bowhead whale, traveled by umiak in summer and by dogsled in winter, and built permanent winter villages of boulders and turf, the roofs supported by the massive jawbones of whales. Lamps and cooking pots were carved from soapstone, a technique they may have learned from the Dorset people, and an improvement on the fragile pottery vessels used by their Alaskan ancestors. They were a metal-using people, acquiring native copper from the Coppermine River area, iron from the iron-rich meteorites of northwestern Greenland and through occasional contacts with the Greenlandic Norse.

This relatively rich way of life was brought to an end across much of the Arctic after about 1600, when maritime hunting was made more difficult by the cold climatic period known as the Little Ice Age, and possibly by a decline in whale stocks brought about by European hunting in the North Atlantic. Only in the relatively warm areas of Alaska, Labrador and southern Greenland, where the Inuit replaced the Norse, was a Thule way of life maintained until the time of European contact. Many areas of arctic Canada were abandoned, and elsewhere the Thule people were forced to adapt their economies to the new conditions. With less emphasis on open-water hunting, most groups began to spend the summers in the interior, fishing and hunting caribou. Unable to store sufficient meat and fuel for winter occupations of permanent houses, they spent winters in snow-house villages while hunting seals at breathing holes and ice leads. The Inuit way of life, as described by early European explorers, was therefore a very recent development, a relatively impoverished adaptation forced on their Thule ancestors by an environment that could no longer support summer whaling and winters spent in idleness and feasting.

Elsewhere in the Arctic, the Little Ice Age must have had similar effects. Across Eurasia, reindeer herding may have become more attractive to northern hunters faced with a diminishing supply of game. This may account for the fact that, as the Russians penetrated Siberia, they encountered many groups of reindeer herders who had recently arrived in the north, displacing the hunting peoples who continued to survive in only a few isolated regions. The penetration of Europeans and European trade goods into the arctic regions of both the Old and New Worlds over the past several centuries also produced changes in the economies and societies of northern peoples.

As a result of these changes, the ways of life of aboriginal arctic peoples, as they were described at the time of European contact, were often quite different and often more impoverished than they had been a few centuries earlier. These ways of life cannot be seen, as they often are, as the result of millenniums of gradual adaptation to an unchanging arctic environment. Rather, they are the result of numerous and complex forces acting in different ways at different times on different human societies, and producing a diversity of ingenious and rewarding adaptations to the accidents of environmental change and historical chance.

TRADITIONAL LIFE

ABOVE *A long-abandoned Hudson's Bay Company post near Tavani on the west coast of Hudson Bay. When the natives lived scattered across the north, the trading company had many small posts. Now all company stores are in the towns and villages of the Arctic.*

RIGHT *After a successful narwhal hunt, Polar Inuit in kayaks return to shore near Thule (Qaanaaq) in northwest Greenland.*

ABOVE *An Inuit family migrates across the fall tundra in search of caribou. Today, such trips are usually made with all-terrain vehicles.*

RIGHT, ABOVE *A Yukaghir baby in a traditional reindeer skin bag at a reindeer herders' camp in Siberia.*

RIGHT, BELOW *Returning from a walrus hunt to Little Diomede Island, U.S.A., in Bering Strait. In the background is Big Diomede Island (Ostrov Ratmanova), U.S.S.R. Little Diomede is one of the last places in the north where natives use umiaks, large, skin-covered boats.*

212

*Nenets reindeer herders on the shore
of the Kara Sea.*

ABOVE *After a successful walrus hunt in spring, Polar Inuit of northwest Greenland use dog teams to haul the heavy carcasses out onto the ice.*

LEFT *A Polar Inuk and his son, of northwest Greenland, eat raw murres shot near the ice edge — a quick, healthy and warming meal.*

OPPOSITE *Long ago, most coastal Inuit had kayaks. Today, they are only used in Greenland. Sometimes, at remote camp sites, bleached skeletons of these elegant boats of former days can be found.*

ABOVE *A Lapp family in full finery near their home in Finnish Lapland. The baby is in a* komsa, *a carrying cradle of ancient design, now rare.*

RIGHT *A Lapp in arctic Norway leads a long string of draft reindeer pulling sleds during the spring migration from his inland winter home to his summer camp on the arctic coast. Many Lapps still make this migration, but most now use snowmobiles, cars or even planes.*

ABOVE *A hunter from Ellesmere Island, Canada, builds an igloo for the night. No longer used as winter dwellings, snow houses are still built as shelters during extended trips, because they are much warmer than tents.*

LEFT *A young resident of the Taymyr Peninsula in traditional dress.*

OPPOSITE *A Polar Inuit woman spreads cleaned narwhal sinew upon a plywood sheet to dry. Sinew makes the best thread known to sew leather boots, clothing and kayak covers.*

OVERLEAF *Tiny among great, frozen-in icebergs, a Polar Inuk of northwest Greenland travels by dog team along a trail from Siorapaluk to hunt at the floe edge.*

ABOVE *Char* (Salvelinus alpinus), *rich in protein and fat, is the finest food fish of the Canadian Arctic. Split, cleaned and air-dried upon racks, it is preserved by Inuit as a valuable winter food.*

RIGHT *Large numbers of Greenland halibut die occasionally beneath the winter ice, and many float into leads where Polar Inuit gaff the dead or dying fish.*

OPPOSITE *Using a* kakivak, *a three-pronged leister and a jigging lure, an Inuk of Repulse Bay in northwest Hudson Bay fishes for lake trout.*

OVERLEAF *An* inukshuk *("that which has the shape of man") in the Northwest Territories.* Inukshuit *were used as markers or to drive caribou toward hidden hunters.*

CHAPTER 13

Polar Exploration

ACADEMICIAN A.F. TRESHNIKOV

A LOOK AT A MAP OF THE ARCTIC brings to mind the many brave men who over the ages have trekked to this harsh region of the earth, their explorations sometimes ending in tragedy. Our knowledge of the Arctic has been obtained at the price of the strenuous efforts of these people and the sacrifices they made. Both attest to man's long-held desire to learn about the enormous resources of the region and to put them to use.

In the past, most of the people who traveled here were attracted by practical pursuits: trade, hunting and fishing, the acquisition of new territories and the exploration of sea routes. During the 11th and 12th centuries, Russians from Novgorod and Rostov-Suzdal, searching for new lands and a freer life, settled along the shores of the arctic seas. They fished and hunted walrus and seal, and came to be known as the *pomors* — literally, "people of the sea." In the 14th century, they were sailing from the White Sea to western Europe, and in the next century, they reached Novaya Zemlya and Spitsbergen (now called Svalbard). Hunting expeditions and trade in furs with local tribes took them as far as the Kara Sea. Here, at the estuary of the Taz River, a large trading post emerged in the 16th century. Called Mangazeya, for many decades it remained a center of Russian fur trade.

In the 16th century, Portugal and Spain, the strongest nations at that time, had a monopoly on the sea routes to India and China, which went around Africa and South America. Enterprising men and trading companies of other European countries were therefore interested in routes that would take them to the Far East via the arctic waters. However, European geographers had only a vague idea of what was at the North Pole. On their maps, this area was marked *Mare Congulatum* ("Frozen Sea").

The seafarers of those days set out in small sailing vessels in search of a sea route around Eurasia (a northeastern passage) or around North America (a northwestern passage). All their expeditions ended in failure, and many of their members died from starvation and exposure. Their wooden sailing ships could not stand up against the formidable ice.

In the 17th century, the more enterprising of the *pomors* and the northern Cossacks (*pomors* who were in the service of the tsar) explored the northern coast of Siberia. They reached it by sailing down Siberian rivers in their boats, or *kochas*, which also took them farther out to the arctic seas. On the riverbanks, the *pomors* built winter settlements, where some of them stayed to collect tribute (*yasak*) from the natives, mostly in the form of arctic fox, sable and squirrel pelts. Others made their home there and married local women. They traded in furs and engaged in trapping and fishing. Gradually, the Russians moved eastward until they reached the Pacific coast; in 1648, an expedition headed by a Cossack, Semyon Dezhnev, sailed around the northeastern tip of Asia and out into the Pacific Ocean.

From 1733 to 1743, seamen of the Great Northern Expedition mapped Eurasia's entire northern coastline. And in 1741, a Russian expedition led by Vitus Bering and Aleksey Chirikov discovered the Pacific coast of Alaska and the Aleutian Islands.

In those days Alaska was called Russian America. At the end of the 18th century, Russian merchants set up the Russian-American Company for the sale of Alaskan furs. On the island of Sitka, Russian colonists founded a town and built a fortress, which they called Novoarkhangelsk. Also at that time, Russian seamen sailed along the Arctic coast of Alaska and mapped its coastline all the way to Point Barrow. The Russian-American Company sent young men who were born in Alaska of marriages between Russians and natives to study at navigation schools in Russia. On their return to Alaska, they explored its coastal areas and farther inland. In 1867, Alaska was sold to the United States for $7,200,000.

The search for a sea route off the North American coast, which began in the 16th century, produced few results. The British and Dutch expeditions led by Martin Frobisher (1576–1578), John Davis (1585–1588), Henry Hudson (1610), William Baffin (1612–1616) and others explored the islands along the Atlantic coast of North America, but the straits and inlets separating these islands were filled with floating ice, making them impassable for sailing vessels. The efforts to find a northwestern route were thus dropped and only resumed 200 years later. In 1845, two power-sail ships under the command of John Franklin were sent by the British Admiralty to find a northwest passage. The expedition never returned. In subsequent years a large number of expeditions set out in search of the Franklin team and in the process explored a number of Canadian arctic islands. The first general survey of the Canadian Arctic was completed from 1898 to 1902 by a Norwegian expedition led by Otto Sverdrup.

A voyage from the Atlantic to the Pacific via the southern straits between the islands of the Canadian archipelago was first accomplished in three seasons from 1903 to 1906 by the Norwegian Arctic explorer Roald Amundsen. This outstanding achievement marked the successful completion of the many-year search for a northwestern route. From a commercial point of view, however, this new route, which lay through shallow, winding, ice-bound straits, was of no value. The United States had already started the construction of the Panama Canal, which was opened to navigation in 1914.

From 1904 to 1911, the Canadian government sent a number of expeditions to the arctic islands. The heads of these expeditions claimed for Canada not only the land where they set foot, but also all the other adjoining islands. During World War II, the *St. Roch*, a Canadian schooner under the command of Henry Larsen, made a northwestern voyage from the Pacific to the Atlantic in two seasons (1940–1942). In 1944, Larsen completed the same voyage in a single season, but from the opposite direction via straits in still more northerly latitudes. From the 1950s, this route has been explored and then used commercially by Canadian and American icebreakers and oil tankers. This was necessitated by the discovery of oil, gas and other minerals in the Canadian arctic archipelago.

The first successful voyage from the Atlantic to the Pacific along the northeastern route, by the coasts of Siberia, was made by the Swedish arctic explorer A.E. Nordenskjöld. He accomplished the journey in one season from 1878 to 1879. All further exploration of the Northeast Passage was done by Russians. Russia regarded this route as being particularly important for exploiting Siberia's natural resources and for establishing a link between the European part of the country and its far eastern territories.

While attempts were being made to sail along a northeastern and a northwestern route, some explorers looked for a route directly across the North Pole. Back in the 17th century, it was thought that the ocean around the Pole was free of ice, because the whalers who hunted near Spitsbergen sailed west of the island as far north as 83° N. Now we know that this vast arctic area is free of ice due to the warm currents of the Gulf Stream. It was also believed then that salt water did not freeze and that the ice in the Arctic Ocean was brought there by rivers. In his

ABOVE *The second Grinnell Expedition in search of Sir John Franklin in winter quarters, 1853.*

LEFT *During A.E. Nordenskjöld's search for the Northeast Passage, a group of Chukchis visited his ship, the* Vega.

The two ships of the Nares expedition fast to the floe in Franklin Pearce Bay, August 9, 1875.

work, *On the Possibility of Navigation through the Siberian Ocean to the East Indies*, the great 18th-century Russian scientist Mikhail Lomonosov wrote: "Away from the Siberian shores, the Siberian ocean is free of ice in the summer months."

In accordance with Lomonosov's ideas, the Russian Admiralty organized an expedition to the Arctic in 1765, which was led by V.Ya. Chichagov. The ships of the expedition twice attempted to reach the northern parts of the Arctic by sailing along the western coast of Spitsbergen, but at 80° N they encountered impassable ice and had to turn back. Subsequent British expeditions confirmed that ships could not reach the North Pole.

The goal of reaching the North Pole provided another incentive for penetrating the central Arctic. Ambitious arctic explorers tried to be the first to hoist the flags of their countries on that remote spot of the globe. In 1827, the Englishman William Parry set out on foot from Spitsbergen, walking on drifting ice floes. However, he was only able to reach 82°45′ N; the drifting ice kept carrying him southward.

In the middle of the 19th century, the German geographer August Petermann revived the idea that there was open sea around the North Pole. He thought that the ice belt ended somewhere north of Spitsbergen and Greenland and that a stretch of ice-free water lay beyond. Two American polar explorers, Elisha Kent Kane (1853–1855) and I.I. Hayes (1860–1861), attempted to reach the "open water" of the Arctic Ocean from Greenland and the Canadian arctic archipelago. Before they were forced to retreat, they saw dark clouds ("watery sky") in the north and were convinced that the part of the Arctic Ocean around the Pole was ice-free.

Mistaken notions often die hard. Again on the basis of Petermann's theory, two German expeditions under Karl Koldeway (1868 and 1869), an expedition led by the American explorer Charles Hall (1871) and one led by the Englishman G.S. Nares (1875–1876) tried sailing northward to reach the North Pole. All failed.

In 1879, an American expedition led by George De Long set out from the Bering Strait on a journey that ended in 1881. De Long did not think there was an ice-free polar sea, but he hoped that the drifting ice would carry his ship to the central parts of the Arctic. The *Jeannette*, hemmed in by ice floes in the Chukchi Sea, drifted for almost two years along the northern edge of the East Siberian Sea before being crushed by ice off the New Siberian Islands. The crew traveled in three lifeboats in the direction of the Lena River. One boat disappeared in the Laptev Sea. Another, with De Long on it, reached the mouth of the Lena, but its crew died of starvation and exposure on one of the islands of the delta. Those in the third boat landed in still another place in the delta and were rescued by local Russians.

Three years after the loss of the *Jeannette*, natives living on the southern shores of Greenland found 50 objects on a small ice floe, among them a food inventory list signed by De Long and a pair of waterproof trousers. The find indicated that there was a constant drift of ice from the East Siberian Sea toward the Greenland Sea across the central Arctic.

After this discovery, the Norwegian scientist Fridtjof Nansen decided to penetrate to the heart of the Arctic by drifting with the ice. He had a ship built to his own design and called it the *Fram*. In the autumn of 1893, Nansen froze his ship into the ice almost exactly where the *Jeannette* had been crushed years before. The *Fram* started a three-year drift, which took it to the Greenland Sea. When he saw that his ship was drifting much farther south than he had expected and was making little progress toward the North Pole, Nansen tried to reach the Pole by dogsled and kayak accompanied by a sailor called Hjalmar Johansen. However, they made it only as far north as 86°14′ N and 95°1′ E and then turned back. The trip over the ice was much too arduous, and their food stock was running low.

The Nansen expedition was a signal event in the history of arctic exploration. It gathered much valuable scientific data and

Fridtjof Nansen and Hjalmar Johansen at the start of their attempt to reach the North Pole.

finally put an end to the myth about an ice-free sea around the North Pole. But since, like others before him, Nansen did not reach the Pole, it continued to lure explorers from many countries. It is generally considered that Robert Peary, an American, first reached the North Pole on April 6, 1909. But just when he declared to the world that he had raised the Stars and Stripes at the Pole, another American, Frederick Cook, claimed that he had reached it a full year earlier on April 21, 1908. Peary promptly called his rival a liar, who had "thought up" his trip to the Pole. Thus began a fierce argument between the supporters of Peary and those of Cook, an argument that has continued even after their deaths.

Some people thought that Frederick Cook had gone a short distance north of Ellesmere Island, but that his account of a trip to the North Pole was imaginary. However, after reading his books, *My Attainment of the Pole* and *Return from the Pole*, it seems inconceivable to me that anyone could have invented the natural phenomena in the central Arctic that he describes.

On its return from the Pole, Cook's party found itself west of its departure point by nearly 100 miles. The assumption in those days was that the ice here drifted eastward. In charting his route, Cook had allowed for this easterly drift, and yet he found himself much farther west than he had expected. This held up Cook's return by almost a year. At the time, he could not explain how this mistake had happened. But years later it was established that the ice in that part of the Arctic drifts not in an easterly direction toward Greenland, but westward, along the shoreline of the Canadian arctic archipelago.

Cook wrote that at about 85° N he had sighted a section of a snow-clad island and that at 88° N he had actually crossed a

The Wakeham expedition raising the Union Jack on Kekerten Island, Northwest Territories, August 17, 1897.

similar island, describing it as a mass of ice with an undulating terrain, which was somewhat higher than the rest of the marine ice. This description was taken as proof that Cook was lying, because there were no islands in the central Arctic. What he was referring to, however, was obviously drifting ice islands, which were discovered after his death. In our day, Soviet and American scientists set up research stations on precisely such "islands."

Today, when hundreds of people have been to the North Pole, and the Soviet atomic icebreaker *Arctika* (renamed *Brezhnev*) sailed there and back in 1977, the question of who was the first to conquer the Pole is of great historical interest. I think that both Robert Peary and Frederick Cook were in the central Arctic somewhere near the North Pole, but it would be wrong to say that they were actually at the Pole. Both were equipped with relatively primitive instruments for charting their routes. For example, they used ordinary pocket-sized magnetic compasses, although it was well known even in those days that the pointers of the magnetic compass are not always reliable in high latitudes. Neither Peary nor Cook could produce convincing proof that he had reached the North Pole. Even a special congressional committee held in 1916 to consider conferring the title of rear admiral upon Peary did not sav that he was the first person to reach the Pole. It simply commended him on the great service he had rendered in the exploration of the Arctic.

In the early 20th century, the Russian explorer V.A. Rusanov attempted to sail along a northeastern route by the Siberian coast. However, his ship disappeared without a trace. A similar expedition was undertaken in 1912 by Captain G.L. Brusilov. When his steamer, the *St. Anna*, entered the Kara Sea, it was gripped by the ice and carried northward and then to the Arctic basin. North of Franz Josef Land, some of the crew left the ship and walked south across the ice. Of the group of 11 men, only 2 survived.

From 1913 to 1915, Russian explorers sailed from the Pacific to the Atlantic along a northern sea route on board the icebreakers *Taimyr* and *Vaigach*. On the 1913 expedition, what turned out to be the last unknown arctic archipelago in the U.S.S.R. — Severnaya Zemlya — and the Vilkitski Strait were discovered.

Twenty-five years after the *Fram* drifted across the Arctic, Roald Amundsen decided to repeat the attempts made earlier by De Long and Nansen to reach the North Pole on board an ice-bound ship. In 1918 he had a special ship built for this purpose. Sailing along the northern sea route, by the Siberian coast, the expedition made its way to Alaska in two seasons. In 1922, in the northern part of the Chukchi Sea, the *Maud* was frozen into the ice and began her drift. The scientists on board carried out important oceanographic research throughout the entire journey. Like the *Jeannette*, the *Maud* was carried along the northern part of the East Siberian Sea, and two years later, in August 1924, she broke clear of the ice at a point north of the New Siberian Islands. Convinced that the ship would not be able to drift closer to the Pole area, the leaders of the expedition (Amundsen did not take part in the drift) decided to return. After spending the winter off Chetyrekhstolbovoi Island, the *Maud* reached Alaska in 1925.

Soon after the 1917 Great October Revolution, Soviet scientists proceeded to carry out systematic research in the Arctic Ocean. On March 10, 1921, Lenin signed a decree on the creation of a Marine Institute (*Plavmornin*), which was to explore the north-ern seas and lands. The institute had a specially equipped ship, the *Perseus*, which was converted from an old wooden whaling and sealing schooner. It was equipped with an ice guard made of oak boards. The activities of the Plavmornin extended to the western seas of the Arctic Ocean. Between 1924 and 1941, the *Perseus* carried out comprehensive oceanographic observa-tions in addition to hunting and biological research.

One year before the Plavmornin was founded, the Presidium of the Supreme National Economic Council issued a decree on the organization of a northern scientific and hunting expedition, which eventually led to the founding of the present Arctic and Antarctic Research Institute. This expedition carried out geolog-ical and biological studies on the Siberian coast. In 1925, it was reorganized into the Institute for the Study of the North. The institute became known worldwide for its part in the rescue of a group of Italians who had survived the crash of the dirigible *Italia*. The rescue operation was carried out from the icebreakers *Krasin* and *Malygin*.

In 1930, the Institute for the Study of the North organized an expedition to explore Severnaya Zemlya. The expedition was headed by Otto Schmidt, and the research group by V.Yu. Vize, who was responsible for the drawing up of an extensive program of geographic and hydro-meteorological study of the northern part of the Kara Sea. An island discovered on the expedition now bears Vize's name. Vize had earlier, on the basis of a study of the records of the *St. Anna*'s drift, put forward the hypothesis that the deflection of this drift in the northern part of the Kara Sea, which was in contradiction to the prevail-ing winds in that area, suggested the presence of an island or at least a large bar. This discovery made "with the help of the pen" was confirmed by the expedition. Three more islands were also discovered.

During the 1930s, in addition to setting up land-based outposts in the Arctic for stationary hydro-meteorological and geophysical observations, a number of oceanographic parties were sent to carry out research on board icebreakers. The study of the Soviet arctic seas was geared to purely practical purposes of navigation. (Shipping along the Northern Sea Route was becoming increasingly important.) Scientists gathered information on ice conditions, currents and the ice drift. They found that the ice conditions of these seas, which are merely gulfs of the Arctic Ocean, depend upon the behavior of the main glacial masses of the ocean.

In 1935, an expedition traveled to the far north on board the icebreaker *Sadko*. The oceanographers probed the depth of the northern part of the Greenland Sea. Samples of the ocean floor lifted from a depth of 9,800 feet were found to contain silt, boulders and bivalves. Geologists and marine scientists established that since the minerals in the boulders and the bivalves were common off the Siberian coast, those found in the Greenland Sea had been brought there by the drifting ice. In the warm waters of the sea, the ice melted, and the foreign matter sank to the bottom.

In later years, the *Sadko* cruised the northern part of the Kara Sea and entered the Arctic basin. At 82°42' N and 87°04' E, the progress of the ship was stopped by perennial ice floes. Here, where the ocean is 7,759 feet deep, oceanographers discovered a thick layer of warm water with a temperature of 36.7°F under a colder upper layer of water with a temperature below 32°F. It was thus established that the warm Atlantic waters sank in the northern part of the Greenland Sea, forming an intermediate deep-sea layer about 1,600 feet thick spread along the entire continental slope of the Arctic basin. A similar warm intermediate layer was discovered in two troughs at the bottom of the northern Kara Sea.

The expeditions of the 1930s proved that it was practically impossible to navigate ships through the thick perennial ice to the center of the Arctic Ocean to carry out research. That is why it was decided to set up a research station on a drifting ice floe. The idea of creating such a station was first suggested in 1924 by Fridtjof Nansen, who organized and headed an international society called Airoarctic. In May 1937, the famous Sever-1 research group (Ivan Papanin, Pyotr Shirshov, Evgeni Fyodorov and Ernst Krenkel) were the first to be airlifted to an ice floe near the North Pole. In a nine-month period, they collected new information about the weather, ice drift and currents, the structure of the water masses, and the geomagnetism and marine life in the depths of the arctic seas, while drifting from the northern geographical Pole to the southern regions of the Greenland Sea.

In the spring of 1941, there were three aircraft landings on drifting ice floes in the region of the Pole of Inaccessibility. A group of scientists from the Arctic Institute for the first time measured the ocean depth in this area, carried out meteorological and geomagnetic observations, measured the temperature of the water at various depths and took samples of the water for chemical tests.

This information provided the basis for the launching after World War II of large-scale research work on ice-based stations in the Arctic, including the expeditions of the Sever series. Every year a new expedition has been airlifted to the arctic ice. The latest in the series is Sever-37, which set out in 1985. As a rule, in the spring, aircraft carrying groups of scientists with portable equipment and instruments touch down at selected spots so that a whole program of oceanographic observations can be completed within several hours. As early as 1948 and 1949, such expeditions discovered the Lomonosov Mountain Range on the ocean floor, and in subsequent years, mapped the relief of the Arctic Ocean floor with its complex mountain chains, deep cracks and gorges. This was particularly important, because prior to 1948 it was thought that the central part of the Arctic Ocean was a deep bowl with a flat bottom. These discoveries are among the greatest geographic discoveries of the 20th century.

From 1950 to 1951 a Severnyi Polyus-2 drifting station (SP-2) headed by M. Somov functioned in the eastern part of the Arctic basin. SP-3 (headed by myself) and SP-4 (headed by E. Tolstikov) were set up in the spring of 1954. Since 1954, at least two Soviet drifting stations have been working on the ice of the Arctic. In addition to oceanographic, meteorological, glaciological and geophysical research, the stations serve as a base for conducting large-scale thermophysical, radiophysical and other types of observations. Several American stations have also operated in the Arctic at different times.

Since 1936, the Arctic Institute has sent out expeditions every year to patrol the ice edge of the arctic seas. At first these ice patrols (as they came to be called) sailed in small motor launches. Later, when it became more effective to collect information on the geographical distribution of ice from the air, the ice patrols began each summer to carry out aerial oceanographic surveys of the ice-free regions of the ocean. As a result of their research, a detailed nomenclature of marine ice was worked out. It was used while establishing an International Ice Nomenclature, which is now used by the World Meteorological Organization.

In recent years, radar systems equipped with infrared radiometers have been used in aerial monitoring of ice conditions in the Arctic. This makes it possible to conduct such observations even at night. Modern meteorological and oceanographic satellites also provide data about ice conditions.

American and Canadian scientists have carried out research in the waters between the islands of the Canadian arctic archipelago, in the coastal waters of the Chukchi Sea and in the Beaufort Sea along the northern shores of Alaska as far as the Mackenzie River. Prior to 1947, ice observations were carried out from ships sailing along the ice edge. Since 1947, the Americans and Canadians have conducted systematic aerial monitoring of ice conditions along established routes all the way up to the North Pole from Alaska and Newfoundland. These aircraft are now equipped with radar systems. From 1965, general surveys of ice conditions in the Arctic Ocean have also been carried out by satellites.

From 1970 to 1974, a group of American researchers carried out special experiments on ice floes in the Beaufort Sea. The use of modern radio-electronic instruments has made it possible to clarify certain details concerning the drift of the marine ice in the Arctic Ocean and the deformation of ice floes due to uneven movement. In 1980, the Americans set up several automatic drifting stations to transmit, via space satellites, data on air temperature and atmospheric pressure. The satellite data on the location of these stations provided important information about the ice drift in the Arctic basin.

We can now say that, on the whole, the natural phenomena in the Arctic Ocean have been better studied than in other, more accessible, parts of the world ocean. Intensive research has also been carried out into many other natural phenomena in the Arctic. For example, the polar zones draw a great deal of heat away from warmer areas of the globe and therefore largely determine air circulation on earth. Climatic fluctuations and the study of the atmosphere, the ocean, the ice and snow cover and their interaction, which affects climate, are among the major problems confronting the international scientific community.

The research and conservation of arctic plant and animal life is another important area of scientific study. Vast arctic regions fall within the national boundaries of countries, and nature conservation here depends upon the regulations of the countries concerned. The arctic zones of the U.S.S.R. and of North America have in recent years become major producers of oil, gas and ores. New cities and new industrial enterprises are going up and pipelines are being laid. As a result of rapid industrial and economic development in the Arctic, sharp changes have oc-

Soviet arctic research station SP-25.

curred in the natural environment near industrial centers and towns. For example, ditches and gullies have appeared where trucks and tractors have worked, and air pollution is destroying trees and shrubs.

The Soviet Arctic is protected by comprehensive nature conservation measures, which are enforced throughout the country. However, the standards for environmental protection originally worked out for climatic zones of the middle latitudes are not necessarily applicable in the Arctic. The low temperature of water and air, the ice and permafrost and other factors create special problems for preserving the arctic ecological systems. Here, chemical and biological self-cleaning processes are very slow. Thus, the permissible level of harmful substances to the environment established for the rest of the country is too high for regions of the Soviet far north. It is necessary to introduce special measures, both on a national and international scale, to protect the natural environment of the Arctic.

I have been working in the field of peaceful exploration of the Arctic for more than 40 years, have made the personal acquaintance of many explorers and researchers from other countries, and have tried to foster and strengthen friendly ties among them. This brief review of the exploration of the Arctic and the scientific problems involved shows that over the ages man has learned a great deal about the natural environment of the Arctic. There is still much to be learned.

Fuel storage tanks, Spence Bay,
Northwest Territories.

CHAPTER 14

A Changing World

DR. ERNEST S. BURCH, JR.

THE PEOPLES OF THE CIRCUMPOLAR NORTH have made the huge leap from the Stone Age to the Modern Age in an incredibly short period of time. Just how short varies from one region to another: in most areas, it has been within a century; in a few, within a single generation. Many authors have commented on this transformation, focusing primarily on broad technological, economic, religious and political changes, but the meeting ground of these and other forces of social change is the family. It is within the family that the conflict between the old and the new is most intense.

Traditionally, the northern family was quite different from the type of family that has been most common in the south. It tended to be much larger, probably averaging around 12 members, and ranging up to 2 or 3 dozen, or even more. However, it was not comprised of one set of parents and their offspring, but of several sets of married adults — usually siblings and cousins and their spouses — their relatively few offspring, and an aged grandparent or two. The typical northern family, regardless of the specific culture concerned, was what anthropologists call an "extended" family.

The members of an extended family usually did not live under one roof, but under several. Two or three couples and their children might live in one house or tent, and their adult siblings and spouses would live in one or more other dwellings very close by. Both adults and children would move between dwellings, and at least the major activities of the whole group would be under the direction of a family head.

Just why couples had so few children is not clear. In a few areas, infanticide was practiced, but usually only during severe famines, and it was rarely common enough to distort population figures. No doubt many children died in infancy or early childhood, just as they did in most other parts of the world before the advent of modern medicine. However, there is reason to believe that northern couples did not have many children in the first place. No one knows why; probably the combination of prolonged breast-feeding, the leanness of the women, and the physical stress associated with nomadism and handling the carcasses of large animals reduced the level of fertility.

Throughout much of the north, extended families constituted entire villages for much of the year. In large, but temporary, seasonal aggregations, or in the few large permanent villages, the houses of the members of each family formed a cluster — in effect, a small neighborhood — within the larger settlement.

As the populations of southern nations expanded, southerners moved into northern regions and established trading posts, missions, schools and administrative centers. Eventually, native populations grew up around these centers. As the amount of migratory movement accordingly declined, the number of offspring born to married couples increased.

At first, the increased birthrates did not make much difference in overall family size, because many of the children died at an early age. When modern medical techniques were applied after World War II, however, the number of surviving children increased dramatically. This put tremendous pressure on extended family households. Each couple was forced to build a separate dwelling simply to house its own offspring. Small outbuildings were sometimes erected to house the aged. Because the same medical revolution that increased the survival rate of the young also increased the survival rate of the elderly, there were more of them to be provided for as well. This demographic revolution, as much as any other factor, has been a source of stress among northern peoples.

Life in a traditional extended family "village" was probably as self-contained as life can be. Day after day, the same few individuals were in contact with one another, but with no one else. The men hunted and fished together, and often worked together making the equipment needed to sustain life. The women gathered in one or two of the dwellings to sew or, if berry picking, cleaning fish or butchering caribou (reindeer) was on the day's agenda, they did that together as well. In the evenings, the entire community gathered in the largest dwelling to eat and perhaps tell stories or play games.

As it proceeded through the seasonal round of movement necessary to harvest the nomadic game animals of the north, the family might divide for a time when food supplies were low. Or, other relatives might come to join the original group. And, among most northern peoples, large aggregations of a few hundred or even a thousand or more people would form for brief periods of feasting and other celebration, usually during the summer. But after a person had reached adulthood and had gone through the seasonal round several times, he or she rarely saw a stranger except in time of war.

Education was not a discrete part of a youngster's life; it was, simply, life. Because the adult to child ratio was nearly one to one in most households, childcare was intense. As they matured, youngsters began to perform various chores and to learn through observation and practice things they needed to know to survive. The demographic revolution made this type of upbringing almost impossible. Traditionally, notions of right and wrong were communicated subtly but persistently through casual conversation, storytelling and example. With ten children, that no longer worked very well. But the parents did not know any other way.

As the demographic revolution was taking place, schools were being built in many of the mission/trading post centers. They provided a safety valve for overloaded households; many of the children could go there for at least part of every day, and, later on, were required to do so. But the training they received in school was in the form, if not the complete substance, of an entirely different culture than the one they experienced at home. Once government, as opposed to mission, schools were established, schooling was also carried out in a different language than the one the children learned at home. Much of what they were taught in school had no apparent relevance to the world as they knew it or as they ever expected it to be. These problems were particularly acute in cases where young natives were sent to boarding schools far from home. This practice has largely stopped in recent years, but was rather common.

The contrast between what children learned in school and what they learned at home combined with the demographic revolution to fragment the formerly cohesive native family life. Many youngsters who were forced to speak English (or French or Danish or Norwegian or Russian) at school, or else not speak there at all, found, after a time, that they could no longer communicate well with their grandparents. This generation gap cut off the young people from the traditions of their people without really substituting anything in their place.

By the time the demographic revolution struck, almost everyone in the north was living more or less full-time in permanent villages. Whereas new dwellings belonging to growing extended families previously would have been erected at the periphery of the family cluster, people now began to find that space already occupied by someone else. The new houses might have to be built on the edge of town, thus destroying the physical proximity that was essential to effective extended family life.

In many respects, of course, the fragmentation of family life is a natural part of the modern world. One's siblings and parents do not live next door — they live across town or hundreds of miles away. One does not work at home, one goes somewhere else to do it. One does not get educated at home, one goes to school. The fragmentation of life is occurring everywhere in the modern world, not just in the Arctic. But people in the north, as in many of the so-called "third world" countries, lack both the cultural heritage and the personal experience required to imbue this new sort of life with the values and sentiments required to sustain it. In a fundamental sense, it contradicts everything their ancestors held to be important.

For many northern native families, life in the new era is spent in a town of 2,000 to 10,000 people; some of the towns in the Soviet north are much larger than that, cities in every sense of the word. The streets, houses and other buildings are laid out in a grid established by a government survey, and many of the comforts of cities much farther south are available.

Houses used to be made as small as possible, usually with single rooms, in order to conserve heat. Fuel — driftwood or timber, which had to be cut by hand, or perhaps sea mammal blubber — was burned in open fires, lamps or, more recently, in inefficient homemade metal stoves. The advent of chain saws and highly efficient, factory-made wood-burning stoves, and of stove oil and propane, has done much to alleviate the heating problem, making it possible to keep even large houses quite warm. Most houses now found in northern towns would not look dramatically out of place in a middle-class neighborhood of a southern city.

The populations of northern communities have increased tremendously over the past 30 years. This is partly because of the centralization of the previously dispersed native population and because of its dramatic growth. It is also due to the influx of non-native southerners. The latter include government workers, doctors, nurses, teachers and store managers almost everywhere and, in regions where major resource development is taking place, often thousands of engineers, miners, truck drivers, laborers and their dependents, as well as the many other types of support personnel required to sustain a major enterprise. In many districts, northern natives now constitute a minority in their own land.

Population growth and the difficulty of providing adequate public services have made housing both difficult to find and very expensive to rent or buy. The solution to the housing problem here, as in the south, is the apartment house. Several can now be found in virtually every northern town having more than 2,000 residents. Just how well people who were born in tiny sod houses — not to mention snow houses or tents — in villages of less than, say, 200 people, adjust to life in a building that contains that number of inhabitants alone remains to be seen.

A crucial factor in adjusting to town life in the north is money, and money can be acquired only through jobs or welfare, whether it be in Canada or the U.S.S.R. Unfortunately, employment in most northern towns tends to be low, seasonal and with little real substance behind it at the local level. Most jobs involve manual labor or service-type work in support of government offices, missions and schools, or in the general infrastructure (post offices, stores, airports) that has grown up to service them. Such jobs are often limited in number.

Over the past generation, as more and more young natives have completed high school and university training, some of them have begun to move up the occupational hierarchy into secretarial or management positions, and some have started businesses of their own. Since more humble jobs are not eliminated by this process, the overall effect is to increase the employment opportunities. In a few regions, mineral or petroleum production, or commercial fishing, has provided a more substantial foundation for the local economy. Recent studies suggest that, no matter how great the change in lifestyle might be, the ability to support oneself and one's family is just as important for the self-esteem of a northern native as it is for a resident of the biggest southern city.

Food preferences appear to be among the more tenacious of traditional habits. Many northern town and city dwellers prefer the food of their ancestors to what is available at the local grocery store. Unfortunately, the larger the town, the more difficult it is for the residents to hunt and fish, not to mention process their harvest in a traditional way. To an amazing degree, however, this problem is being overcome through the use of powerful motorboats, snowmobiles, aircraft and all-terrain vehicles. These enable hunters to hunt over an immense area in a short amount of time and to bring their harvest home. The custom of having family hunting camps outside of town has also been revived in recent years, particularly in Canada and Alaska. People with full-time jobs can speed the hundred miles or so out to their camp after work on Friday, spend the weekend there engaged in traditional subsistence pursuits in the company of their close kin, and be back in town Sunday night.

Another major source of native food is the small, predominantly native village of 150 to 500 people, several hundred of which remain in the circumpolar north. Even here, television, large prefabricated houses, heating oil, modern schools, telephones and electricity have become nearly universal. Property lines and zoning restrictions all but prohibit the formation of new extended family neighborhoods or the extension of old ones, but in spite of this, traditional extended families somehow persist and often flourish in these villages.

Nowadays, although parents and their adult offspring may live in houses located some distance apart, the men often hunt (or fish or herd reindeer) together, the women pick berries together, and they all distribute a portion of their harvest to any family member who needs it. They also share financial resources. There is an increasingly well-developed pattern in some village families in which some of the younger, better-educated people get jobs, when they can, while the older ones continue to hunt, fish or herd reindeer for food. When they pool the results of their labors, everyone's basic needs are satisfied. And when a surplus of native food has been acquired, it is given or sold to people in the larger towns.

Even the leaders are showing an interesting return to older patterns. Traditionally, men in their forties or fifties tended to be in charge. Then, a generation or two ago, many young people who had acquired some fluency in the dominant non-native language, as well as some experience in dealing with outsiders, were thrust to the fore. However, many of these same individuals remain in leadership positions today. They are now in their forties and fifties, which, had they been leaders many generations ago, is the age they would have been. The new arctic native leaders in North America and Scandinavia formed pressure groups, ran for public office, initiated legal proceedings and generally fought for what they thought was rightfully theirs. The main thing they fought for was control of the land that their ancestors had occupied since before the arrival of Europeans.

Given the number, variety and power of the forces that have torn northern people from their traditional ways of life, it should come as no surprise to find that many are confused and that alcoholism and suicide rates are very high. What is amazing is that they have retained any sense of purpose at all. Much of this is due to the remarkable tenacity of traditional family values of mutual support and courage in the face of adversity. The future is unknown, but there is no doubt that in most countries northern natives are more in control of their own affairs now than they have been for several generations. Given this success, and their desire to remain in their traditional homelands, there is every reason to believe that their futures will be secure.

244

MODERN LIFE

ABOVE *The nuclear-powered ice-breaker* Brezhnev *pilots a caravan of ships through the Kara Sea.*

LEFT *At the end of winter on the Chukchi Sea. Snowmobiles have become a popular method of transport throughout the arctic world.*

The Anglican church in Cape Dorset,
Northwest Territories, in 1971.

ABOVE *By 1982, the same church is no longer outside the town.*

RIGHT *A Polar Inuit elder reads the Bible at a service.*

*The town of Cape Dorset, Northwest
Territories, in February.*

ABOVE *The modern Inuit village of Lake Harbour on southern Baffin Island. A marker on a hill indicates distances to various parts of the world.*

RIGHT, ABOVE *Yakutsk, Siberia, street-scene. Yakutsk, on the left bank of the Lena River, is the capital city of the republic of Yakutia.*

RIGHT, BELOW *Murmansk, on the Kola Gulf, is an ice-free port kept open all winter by the warm Gulf Stream.*

ABOVE *This apartment block in Siberia is just one of many being built across the Arctic.*

LEFT *A girl from Little Diomede Island, Alaska.*

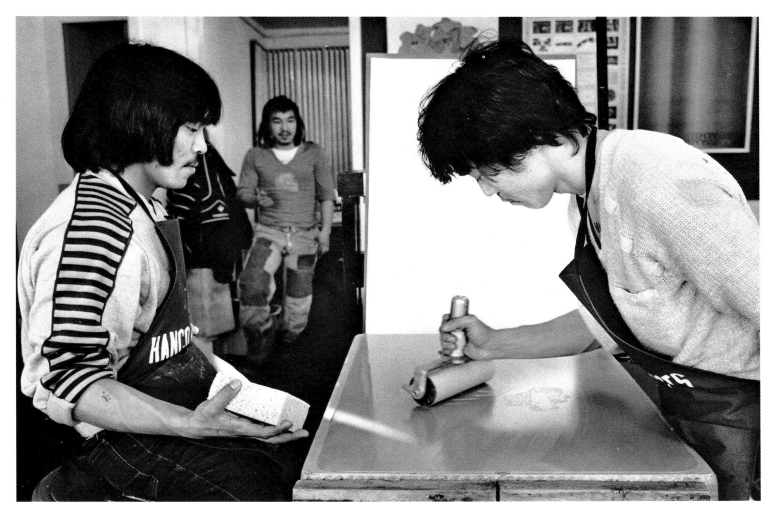

ABOVE *Printing pressmen in Cape Dorset, Canada, where there is a thriving community of artists.*

RIGHT *A Canadian Inuit couple on their wedding day.*

ABOVE *Scientists of the Arctic Biological Station inflate a balloon on northern Somerset Island, Canada, to photograph large pods of white whales in a nearby inlet.*

RIGHT *Russian archaeologists study artifacts from an ancient native settlement on Wrangel Island.*

Index

ALASKA
  Highway, 136
  history of, 21, 23, 117, 119-21, 136, 204, 226
  mining in, 135, 138-40
  Native Claims Settlement, 139
  native peoples of, 25-26, 55, 58, 61, 126, 133
  Pipeline, 138-39
Aleuts, 61, 119, 120, 126
Amundsen, Roald, 133, 227, 232-33
Animals, 25, 29, 32, 163-69 *See also individual species*
  prehistoric, 50-51, 54-55
Arctic
  animals, 25, 29, 32, 50-51, 54-55, 163-169
  biomes, 27
  birds, 21, 32, 164, 165, 166, 167
  climate, 26, 27, 29, 49, 57, 87, 144, 172, 207, 208, 236
  environmental concerns in, 141, 143, 236-37
  exploration, 81, 96, 123-24, 127-31, 225-34
  geology, 29
  hydropower, 140
  mining, 93-94, 135, 136, 138-40, 144, 227
  peoples, 19, 20, 25-26, 29, 239-44
  plants, 29, 32, 171-76
  prehistory, 49-55, 61-62, 64, 201-08
  strategic importance of, 136
  tourism, 143
Arctic Ocean, 230, 232, 234, 235, 236
Auklet, least, 32

BAFFIN, William, 123-24
Baranov, Aleksandr, 120
Barents, Willem, 94
Barren Grounds, 20, 57
Bear, polar, 81-82, 86, 144, 164, 165-66
Bering, Vitus, 54, 116-19, 226
Beringia, 54, 201, 202
Birds, 21, 32, 164, 165, 166, 167. *See also individual species*
Boreal forest, 26, 27, 29

Britain, exploration of Arctic by, 91-96, 126-30, 226, 229
Burrough, Stephen, 93
Bylot, Robert, 123

CANADA, arctic. *See also* Labrador, Newfoundland
  exploration of by Canada, 227
  history of, 92, 96, 121, 124, 203
  mining in, 138
  native peoples of, 20, 26, 58, 125, 126, 135, 136-37, 138.
Caribou, 29, 163-64. *See also* Reindeer
  hunting of, 58, 60
Catherine II, Empress, 119
Chancellor, Richard, 92
Chichagov, V. Ya, 229
Chukchis, 29, 49
Climate, 26, 27, 29, 49, 57, 87, 144, 172, 207, 208, 236
Cook, Frederick, 231-32
Cro-Magnon people, 53

DAVIS, John, 94
De Long, George, 230
Dezhnev, Semyon, 115, 226
Diomede Islands, 25-26, 31
Dogs, arctic, 166, 167
Dovekie, 32
Drifting research stations, 234, 235
Duck, eider, 167

EGEDE, Hans, 125
Eirik the Red, 86-87
Evenks, 57

FISHING, 125
Fort Ross, 120
Franklin, Sir John, 130, 226
Frobisher, Martin, 64, 93

GERMANY, exploration of Arctic by, 230
Greenland, 19, 136
  Danish rule of, 125-26, 143-44
  mining in, 136
  native peoples of, 87, 125, 128-29, 135, 136

Norse settlements of, 86-88
  prehistory of, 204
Gyrfalcon, 84

HARE, arctic, 31
Hayes, I.I., 230
Hearne, Samuel, 57
Holland
  exploration of Arctic by, 94, 226
  whaler-traders of, 124-25
Hudson, Henry, 94, 96, 123
Hudson's Bay Company, 92, 96, 121, 124, 130
Hunting
  of caribou, 58, 203
  prehistoric methods of, 52, 53, 55, 62, 202, 204-05, 207
  of sea mammals, 58, 62, 96, 124, 129, 133

ICE, 235-36
Ice ages, 49, 50, 53
  Little Ice Age, 128, 208
Icebergs, 84
Iceland, 84, 86
Igloo, 62, 137, 205
Inuit, 29, 49, 61, 62, 137-39, 144, 207
  American, 25-26, 55, 58, 61, 126, 133
  Canadian, 20, 26, 58, 126, 133, 136-37, 138
  Greenland, 19-20, 26, 125, 127-29, 136, 138
  Soviet, 25-26
Ivan IV, Tsar, 92, 113

JOHNSON, Richard, 93

KAMCHATKA Peninsula, 118
Kane, Elisha Kent, 230
Kayak, 62, 137
Kodlunarn Island, 93
Komsas, 206

LABRADOR, 26, 125-26, 203
Lapps, 19, 29, 57, 58, 83, 204
Larsen, Henry, 227

255

Leif the Lucky, 88
Lemmings, 31, 165
Lerner, Theodor, 23
Lofoten Islands, 172
Longyear, John, 136

MAMMOTH, 50-51, 54, 55, 82
Mining, 93-94, 135, 136, 138-40, 144, 227
Moravian Brethren, 125-26
Muscovy Company, 92
Musk-ox, 54, 163

NANSEN, Fridtjof, 133, 230-31, 234
Narwhal, 82, 87
Native peoples. See also Alaska, Canada,
  Siberia, individual peoples
  education of, 241
  family life, traditional, 239-43
  food of, 243-44
  houses of, 240, 242, 243
  prehistory of, 201-08
Neanderthal people, 51-53
Nenets, 58
Newfoundland, 84, 88
Nordenskjöld, A.E., 133, 227
Norse people, 60, 82-83, 86-88
Northeast Passage, 91-93, 133, 226, 227
North Pole, 130, 227-32
North Water, 123
Northwest Passage, 91, 93, 94, 96, 123-24,
  126-30, 133, 144, 226, 227
Northwest Territories. See Canada
Norway, 23, 86, 172, 203. See also
  Svalbard
  exploration of Arctic by, 133, 227

OTTAR, 60, 82-83

PALEOESKIMOS, 61, 62, 88, 204-07
Parry, William, 126-27, 130, 229
Paul I, Tsar, 120
Peary, Robert E., 20, 130, 231-32
Permafrost, 29, 171
Peter I, Tsar, 115
Petermann, August, 229
Plants
  flowering, 173-74, 176
  grasses, 172, 173, 174, 175, 176
  growth of, 29, 32, 171-72, 174, 175-76
  herbaceous broad-leaved, 172, 173, 176
  lichens, 27, 32, 173, 174
  mosses, 27, 172
  sedges, 175, 176
  shrubs, 172, 173, 174, 176
  treeline, 171
  trees, 27, 171, 172, 173
Polar desert, 173, 174, 176
Polar Inuit. See Inuit, Greenland
Ptarmigans, 164, 165
Pytheas, 81

RAE, John, 130
Reindeer, 163-64, 169. See also Caribou
  herding of, 58, 60-61, 206
  pounds, 60
Ross, John, 126-29
Rusanov, V.A., 232
Russia. See Siberia

Russian-American Company, 120, 121,
  226

SAAMI. See Lapps
Sable, 29, 115
Saint Brendan, 84
Schmidt, Otto, 233
Seals, 164-65, 169
Sea otter, 119, 121
Severin, Timothy, 84
Seward, William H., 23
Shelekhov, Grigori, 119
Siberia
  cities of, 242
  exploration of, 115-17, 226, 232, 233
  fur wealth of, 114-15
  history of, 113, 119, 124, 135, 202, 203,
  205, 208, 225, 226
  industry in, 135, 141, 236-37
  mining in, 140
  native peoples of, 57, 58, 60
  reindeer herding in, 60, 208
Simpson, Sir George, 121
Snow, 29
Snow house, 62, 137, 205
Spitsbergen, 23, 96, 136
Squirrels, ground, 165
Stefansson, Vilhjalmur, 20, 130, 139
Steller, Georg Wilhelm, 118-19
Steller's sea cow, 54, 119
Svalbard, 23, 96, 136
Sverdrup, Otto, 23, 131, 227
Sweden, 58
  exploration of Arctic by, 133

TAIGA, 27, 29, 172
Trans-Siberian Railroad, 135
Treeline, 27, 171, 172-73
Trees, 171, 172, 173
Tundra, 27, 29, 31, 171, 172, 173

UMIAK, 25, 64, 137
U.S.S.R. See Siberia
United States. See Alaska
Utkuhikhalingmiut, 20

VIZE, V. Yu., 233
von Wrangel, Baron Ferdinand, 121

WALRUS, 23, 82, 164-65
  arctic, 27
Whales, 164-65, 169
  bowhead, 94, 96, 133
Whaling, 96, 124, 127, 129, 133
Willoughby, Sir Hugh, 92

YAKUTS, 57
Yermak, 114